麦格希 中英双语阅读文库

校园幽默故事
在快乐中成长
第1辑

【美】麦瑟尔德 (Ken Methold) ●主编

张琳琳 ●译

麦格希中英双语阅读文库编委会 ●编

全国百佳图书出版单位
吉林出版集团股份有限公司

图书在版编目（CIP）数据

校园幽默故事. 第1辑, 在快乐中成长 /(美) 麦瑟尔德 (Ken Methold) 主编; 张琳琳译; 麦格希中英双语阅读文库编委会编. —— 2版. —— 长春: 吉林出版集团股份有限公司, 2018.3（2022.1重印）
（麦格希中英双语阅读文库）
ISBN 978-7-5581-4738-8

Ⅰ.①校… Ⅱ.①麦… ②张… ③麦… Ⅲ.①英语—汉语—对照读物②故事—作品集—美国—现代 Ⅳ.①H319.4：Ⅰ

中国版本图书馆CIP数据核字(2018)第046447号

校园幽默故事　第1辑　在快乐中成长

| 编　　　　：麦格希中英双语阅读文库编委会
| 插　　　画：齐　航　李延霞
| 责任编辑：沈丽娟
| 封面设计：冯冯翼
| 开　　　本：660mm×960mm　1/16
| 字　　　数：237千字
| 印　　　张：10.5
| 版　　　次：2018年3月第2版
| 印　　　次：2022年1月第2次印刷

| 出　　　版：吉林出版集团股份有限公司
| 发　　　行：吉林出版集团外语教育有限公司
| 地　　　址：长春市福祉大路5788号龙腾国际大厦B座7层
| 电　　　话：总编办：0431-81629929
| 发行部：0431-81629927　0431-81629921(Fax)
| 印　　　刷：北京一鑫印务有限责任公司

ISBN 978-7-5581-4738-8　　定价：38.00元
版权所有　　侵权必究　　举报电话：0431-81629929

前言 PREFACE

英国思想家培根说过：阅读使人深刻。阅读的真正目的是获取信息，开拓视野和陶冶情操。从语言学习的角度来说，学习语言若没有大量阅读就如隔靴搔痒，因为阅读中的语言是最丰富、最灵活、最具表现力、最符合生活情景的，同时读物中的情节、故事引人入胜，进而能充分调动读者的阅读兴趣，培养读者的文学修养，至此，语言的学习水到渠成。

"麦格希中英双语阅读文库"在世界范围内选材，涉及科普、社会文化、文学名著、传奇故事、成长励志等多个系列，充分满足英语学习者课外阅读之所需，在阅读中学习英语、提高能力。

◎难度适中

本套图书充分照顾读者的英语学习阶段和水平，从读者的阅读兴趣出发，以难易适中的英语语言为立足点，选材精心、编排合理。

◎精品荟萃

本套图书注重经典阅读与实用阅读并举。既包含国内外脍炙人口、耳熟能详的美文，又包含科普、人文、故事、励志类等多学科的精彩文章。

◎功能实用

本套图书充分体现了双语阅读的功能和优势，充分考虑到读者课外阅读的方便，超出核心词表的词汇均出现在使其意义明显的语境之中，并标注释义。

鉴于编者水平有限，凡不周之处，谬误之处，皆欢迎批评教正。

我们真心地希望本套图书承载的文化知识和英语阅读的策略对提高读者的英语著作欣赏水平和英语运用能力有所裨益。

丛书编委会

Contents

A Difficult Question
一个难题 / 1

The Hole In the Ground
地上的坑 / 3

Quick Thinking
敏捷的思维 / 5

The New Doctor
新医生 / 8

A Sad Story
伤心的故事 / 20

The Best Salesman In the World
世界上最优秀的推销员 / 23

Your Need Is Greater Then Mine
你比我更需要 / 26

A Cheap Meal
便宜的午餐 / 11

Not A Small Problem
大问题 / 14

The Package
邮包 / 17

A Very Important Person
大人物 / 29

Violin Lesson
小提琴课程 / 32

Not So Stupid
并不笨 / 35

No Elephants
没有大象 / 38

How Wars Begin
战争是怎样开始的 / 41

The Diet
节食 / 44

A Holiday From School
逃学 / 47

Love Letters
情书 / 49

Quick Service
高效率的服务 / 52

The Umbrella Man
偷伞的人 / 56

Fishing Can Be Dangerous
钓鱼的麻烦 / 57

The Earthquake
地震 / 51

A Family Secret
家族秘密 / 63

No Point
没意思 / 66

Long Life
长寿 / 69

The Bank Robber
银行劫匪 / 72

The Big Baby
大婴儿 / 75

In the Air
坐飞机 / 78

On Guard
站岗 / 81

The Cheater
作弊者 / 84

The Three Tortoises
三只乌龟 / 87

An Old Friend
老朋友 / 90

Not Here
不在这里 / 93

A Bad Doctor
不称职的医生 / 96

Nothing To Complain About
没什么可抱怨的 / 99

A Good-Bye Gift
告别的礼物 / 103

Good Value
物有所值 / 105

Not Funny
无趣 / 108

The Right Tools For the Job
看病需要的工具 / 111

Paid In Full
全单照付 / 114

The Wrong Question
错误的问题 / 117

Bananas Are Bad for You
坏香蕉 / 121

Big John
大约翰 / 123

The Wrong Medicine
吃错药 / 126

Something in the Ear
耳朵里的东西 / 129

Counting Chickens
数小鸡 / 133

A Housing Problem
住房困难 / 135

Dirty Hands
脏手 / 138

The Guitar Player
吉他手 / 141

School Days
上课日 / 144

Importance
人的重要性 / 147

Nothing Unusual
没什么奇怪的 / 150

Free Tickets
免费票// 152

A Fishy Story
关于鱼的故 / 155

Lasting a Lifetime
能用一辈子的手表 / 158

A Difficult Question

Four girls went to school every day by taxi.

One day one of the girls said, "There's a test this morning. Let's get to school late. Then we won't have to take the test."

"What can we tell the teacher?" one of the girls said. "He'll be *angry*. We'll need a good *excuse*."

一个难题

有四个女孩每天都坐出租车去上学。

一天,一个女孩说:"早晨有考试,我们晚点去学校,那样就不用考试啦。"

"可怎么跟老师解释呢?"另一个女孩说,"他会生气的,咱们得找个合理的借口。"

---

angry *adj.* 生气的;愤怒的   excuse *n.* 借口;理由

CULTURE SERIES

The girls thought for several moments, then one of them said, "Let's tell him that our taxi had a *flat tire*."

"That's a good idea," the other girls said. "We'll tell him that."

They arrived at school an hour later. The test was *finished*.

"Why are you late?" the teacher asked. "You missed the test."

"Our taxi had a flat tire," one of the girls said.

The teacher thought for a moment, then he said, "Sit down, one of you in each corner of the room."

The four girls did this.

Then the teacher said, "Write the answer to this question on a piece of paper: Which tire was flat?"

女孩们想了一会,其中一个说:"那我们就告诉老师,乘坐的出租车轮胎漏气了。"

"好主意!"其他的女孩说,"我们就这么说。"

结果她们迟到了一个小时。考试已经结束了。

"你们为什么迟到呢?" 老师问,"你们已经错过了考试。"

"我们乘坐的出租车爆胎了,"其中一个女孩说。

老师想了一会,说:"你们四人各坐一个墙角。"

四个女孩照做了。

接着,老师说:"在纸上回答一个问题:是哪个轮胎爆了?"

---

flat tire 爆胎

finish *v.* 结束

2

The Hole
In the Ground

There was once a farmer who lived near a road.

It was not a busy road, but from time to time, cars passed the farm.

Near the farm gate, there was a large hole in the road.

This hole was always full of water, and the drivers of the cars could not

地上的坑

路边曾经住着一个农夫。

虽然这并不是繁华路段,但不时地总有车经过农场。

农场门前的道路上有个大坑。

坑里总装满了水,司机们看不清水究竟有多深,他们以为可能很浅。

CULTURE SERIES

see how *deep* the hole was. They thought it was probably *shallow*.

Then when they drove into the hole, they could not drive out because it was so deep.

The farmer did not spend much time working on his farm. He spent most of it watching the hole.

When a car drove into it, he pulled the car out with his *tractor* and *charged* the driver a lot of money for doing this.

One day, the driver of a car said to him, "You must make a lot of money pulling cars out of this hole night and day."

"Oh, no," the farmer said. "I don't pull cars out of the hole at night. At night I *fill* the hole with water."

但一旦当他们驶进大坑就出不来了，因为这坑太深了。

农夫在农场里劳作的时间并不长，因为他大部分时间都在盯着那个坑。

当有车掉进坑里时，他就用拖拉机把车拉出来，然后要求司机付一笔钱。

一天，一个司机对他说："你日夜都在这里帮着拉车，挣不少钱了吧。"

"不，"农夫回答说："我晚上不拉车，我得往坑里灌水。"

---

deep *adj.* 深的
tractor *n.* 拖拉机
fill *v.* 注满；装满

shallow *adj.* 浅的
charge *v.* 要价；收费

3

Quick Thinking

One day, Tony met his friend Alan in the street. Tony was quite rich, but Alan was poor. The two boys walked along the street together.

They talked about many things. Tony liked to listen to music and he told Alan about some new songs. Alan liked reading, and he told Tony about some new books.

敏捷的思维

有一天，托尼在大街上碰到了他的朋友艾伦。托尼特别有钱，可艾伦却很穷。两人便一起在大街上走着。

他们谈了很多事。托尼喜欢听音乐，于是给艾伦推荐了一些新歌。艾伦喜欢阅读，也给托尼推荐了一些新书。

CULTURE SERIES

They had the same friends, and they talked about these too.

Then Tony remembered something. "I *lent* you ten dollars last week," he said. "Can you give it back to me?"

"I'm very sorry, Tony," Alan said. "I forgot about it."

Alan thought about this money for a minute. Then he said, "I haven't got any money with me today. I'll pay you back tomorrow."

"All right," Tony said, "I can wait another day."

At that moment a man ran up. He had a knife in his hand. Alan and Tony were afraid. He was a *dangerous* man.

"Give me your money," he said to Tony.

Tony took out his *wallet* and gave it to the *thief*.

他们有相同的朋友，又谈了谈这些朋友。

突然，托尼想起了什么。"我上周借给你10美元，"他说，"你能先还我吗？"

"不好意思，托尼。"艾伦说，"我忘了。"

艾伦想了一会，说："我今天没有带钱，明天还给你吧。"

"好的。"托尼说，"但是不能再晚了。"

正在这时，突然有个人跑过来。手里还拿把刀。他俩都很害怕。那人看起来非常危险。

"把钱交出来，"那人对托尼喊道。

托尼把钱包拿出来给了强盗。

---

lend *v.* 借给；借出
wallet *n.* 钱包；皮夹

dangerous *adj.* 危险的
thief *n.* 窃贼；小偷

◆ QUICK THINKING

The thief took out the money and threw the wallet on to the ground.

"Now you give me your money," he said to Alan.

Alan thought quickly. He took out his wallet, but he did not give it to the thief. He gave it to Tony and said, "I *owe* you some money, Tony. Here it is."

强盗把钱拿出来后就把钱包扔在了地上。

"现在轮到你了。"强盗对艾伦喊道。

艾伦灵机一动，拿出钱包，但没给强盗，而是给了托尼，还说："托尼，我欠你的钱都在这里。"

---

owe *v.* 欠（款）；负（债）

CULTURE SERIES

4

The New Doctor

An old man visited a new doctor, who was very young.

"I don't feel well, doctor," he said. "Please find out what's wrong with me."

"Take off your clothes and lie on the bed," the young doctor said, "I'll *examine* you."

新医生

一个老人去拜访一位年轻的新医生。

"我不舒服,医生。"他说,"帮我检查检查吧。"

"脱了衣服躺在床上。"年轻的医生说,"我给你检查检查。"

---

examine *v.* 检查

THE NEW DOCTOR

The old man took off his clothes and lay down on the bed, and the young doctor examined him. However, he couldn't find anything wrong with the old man.

He listened to his heart. He looked into his *throat*. He examined every part of him.

At last he said, "I'm sorry, but I can't find anything wrong with you. You're as *healthy* as I am."

"That's very strange," the old man said, "because I feel really bad."

"Come back tomorrow and see me again if you don't feel better," the young doctor said. "I'll examine you again."

"All right, doctor," the old man said.

老人把衣服脱了躺在床上，年轻的医生为他做了检查。但却没查出什么毛病。

医生听了听心跳，看了看喉咙，检查了他身体的每个部位。

最后，他说："不好意思，我没发现任何问题。你跟我一样健康。"

"那就奇怪了。"老人说，"因为我真的觉得很不舒服啊。"

"明天再来复诊吧，看看到时会不会好点。"年轻的医生说，"我会再为你做一次检查。"

"好的，医生。"老人说。

---

throat *n.* 喉咙　　　　　　　　　　　healthy *adj.* 健康的

CULTURE SERIES

Slowly, he stood up and put on his clothes. Then he walked out of the hospital.

A few seconds *later*, the doctor's nurse ran in.

"Doctor! Doctor!" she cried. "That man you said was healthy has just died outside the door."

The doctor thought quickly.

"Then turn the body around so that people will think he was coming in," he said.

老人慢慢地站起身，把衣服穿上。然后走出了医院。

几秒钟后，护士突然跑进来。

"医生！医生！"她喊道，"刚才你说很健康的那个老人突然在门外死了。"

医生灵机一动。

"把尸体调一下头，那样别人就以为他正准备进来呢。"他说。

---

later *adv.* 随后；稍后

A Cheap Meal

A man went into a restaurant and sat down at one of the tables.

A *waiter* went up to him and gave him the *menu*.

The man read it carefully, then ordered all the most expensive dishes.

便宜的午餐

一个男人走进一家餐厅，找了张桌子坐了下来。

服务生立即迎上去，递上菜单。

他仔细阅读后点了最贵的菜。

---

waiter *n.* 男服务员   menu *n.* 菜单

CULTURE SERIES

The waiter served the *meal* and the man ate it with great *enjoyment*.

Then a small boy came into the restaurant and sat at the man's table.

The waiter came up and said to the man, "What would your little boy like, sir?"

"Oh, just an ice cream," the man told him. Then he stood up and said to the waiter, "I'm just going out to buy a newspaper."

He left the restaurant. The waiter gave the boy an ice cream. The boy ate it, and then stood up and walked to the door.

The waiter ran towards him.

"Excuse me," he said, "but your father hasn't come back and he

---

服务生一直伺候他用餐，这个人吃得很开心。
突然有个小孩跑过来，坐在桌旁。
服务生过来问："需要给这位小朋友点什么吗？"
"一个冰激凌就够了。"他说完站起身，对服务生说，"我出去买份报纸。"
他离开了餐厅，服务员给小男孩上了一份冰激凌，男孩吃完转身就出去了。
服务生跑向他。
"对不起，"他说，"你爸爸还没回来，他还没为他的午餐和你的冰

---

meal *n.* 一顿饭；一餐   enjoyment *n.* 愉快；快乐

◆ A CHEAP MEAL

hasn't paid for his meal or for your ice cream."

"I'm sorry," the young boy said, "that has nothing to do with me."

"Oh, yes it does," the waiter said. "You will stay here until your father comes back and *pays* his bill."

"He's not my father," the boy said. "I don't know who he is."

The waiter did not understand. "What do you mean?" he asked.

"The man came up to me in the street," the boy said. "He asked me if I liked ice cream. I told him I did. Then he told me to come into the restaurant at 2 o'clock and sit down at his table. He said he'd give me some."

激凌买单呢？"

"不好意思，"小男孩回答道，"那跟我没有关系啊。"

"当然有关系啦，"服务生说，"你必须待在这里，等你爸爸回来买单。"

"他不是我爸爸，"小男孩说，"我根本不知道他是谁啊。"

这把服务生弄糊涂了。"你什么意思啊？"他问。

"那个人在街上找到我，"小男孩说，"问我想不想吃冰激凌，我说想。他便让我两点钟时来这家餐厅，坐在他的桌前，这样就会有冰激凌吃了。"

---

pay *v.* 付钱

CULTURE SERIES

6

Not A Small Problem

Mr Guppy was a very large man. He had a *loud voice* and a bad *temper*. He was not a *giant*, but he was much bigger than most men.

Life was not easy for Mr Guppy. He could seldom find clothes big enough. His feet

大问题

盖皮先生长得很高大。不仅嗓门大，脾气也坏。虽然他并不是个巨人，但比常人高大很多。

可生活对他来说异常艰难，他很少能找到合身的衣服和鞋子。

---

loud *adj.* 大声的；吵闹的
temper *n.* 脾气；性情

voice *n.* 声音；嗓音
giant *n.* 巨人

◆ NOT A SMALL PROBLEM

were too large for most shoes.

In buses, trains and planes, he could not stand up straight. The *roofs* were too low.

In cars he could not move his legs. There was not enough room. At home, his bed was too short. Chairs were always too small.

In fact, wherever he went and whatever he did, Mr Guppy had problems because of his size.

These problems were so bad that Mr Guppy stayed at home most of the time. Life was easier at home.

Then one day, a friend said, "You spend too much time at home. You should go out more. There's a good movie at the theater."

"I can't sit in theater seats," Mr Guppy said. "I'm too big."

"That is no problem," his friend said. "I'll buy you two tickets. You

---

不管在公交车上、火车上、还是飞机上，他都站不直，因为棚顶太低了。

在轿车里，他也动弹不了，因为没有足够的空间。而家里的床也太短了，椅子也太小了。

事实上，不管到哪里或做什么事，他都会因为身材的原因遭遇很多麻烦。这使他大部分时间都得待在家里，因为在家的生活会相对轻松些。

一天，一个朋友对他说："你待在家的时间太长了，应该多出去走走。现在正上映一部好电影呢。"

"可电影院的椅子我坐不下啊，"盖皮先生说，"我个子太大了。"

"没问题，"他朋友说，"我给你买两张票。你去电影院取。"

---

roof *n.* 屋顶；车顶

in fact 事实上

CULTURE SERIES

can get them at the theater when you go."

The friend *reserved* two tickets for Mr Guppy. When the day came, Mr Guppy put on his best clothes and went to the theater.

"You have two tickets for me," he said to the woman in the ticket office. "My name is Guppy."

"Oh, yes, Mr guppy," the woman said. "Here you are, seats G4 and P12. I'm sorry, you and your friend can't sit together because we are very full this evening."

Poor Mr Guppy. He smiled sadly, walked out of the theater and went home.

朋友为他预留了两张票。那天,盖皮先生穿上最帅气的衣服去电影院了。

"给我两张电影票。"他对售票的妇女说,"我叫盖皮。"

"哦,盖皮先生。"妇女说,"给你,G4号和P12号。很抱歉,由于今晚人太多,都满座了,你和你朋友不能挨着坐了。"

可怜的盖皮先生!他苦笑着,走出电影院回家了。

---

reserve *v.* 预留;保留

The Package

One morning a *mailman* walked up to a house. He rang the bell.

A few seconds later a window of the house opened, and a woman put her head out.

"What is it?" she wanted to know.

邮包

一天早晨,邮差来到一户人家,按响了门铃。

几秒钟后,一扇窗户开了,一位妇女探出头来。

"什么事啊?"妇女问。

---

mailman *n.* 邮递员

CULTURE SERIES

"I've got a *package* for Mrs Smith," the mailman said.

"Is it *registered*?" the woman asked.

"Yes," the mailman said.

"Is it a big package or a small package?" the woman wanted to know next.

"It's quite a small package," the mailman told her.

"I see."

The woman thought for a minute, then she said, "Who is it from?"

The mailman looked at the *return address* on the back of the package.

"有个给史密斯太太的邮包。"邮差说。

"是挂号的吗？"妇女问。

"是。"邮差答道。

"是个小的还是大的啊？"妇女还想知道。

"很小的一个。"邮差回答道。

"我知道了。"

妇女想了一会儿，说："谁寄来的？"

邮差看了看邮包背面的邮寄地址。

---

package *n.* 包；包裹　　　　　　　　　　　register *v.* 登记；记名
return address　回信地址

◆ THE PACKAGE

"It's from Jones and Jones in London," he said.

Now the woman was very interested. "From Jones and Jones, eh?" she said. "That's a very *expensive* shop. What's in the package?"

"Madam," the mailman said, becoming quite angry with the woman, "I don't know. Why don't you come down and take the package from me. Then you can open it and *find out*."

"Oh, I can't do that," the woman said.

"Why not?" the mailman asked.

"Because I'm not Mrs Smith," she said. "You've come to the wrong house. Mrs Smith lives next door."

"是伦敦的琼斯寄来的。"他说。

妇女越来越感兴趣了。"是琼斯的?"她说,"那可是一家非常昂贵的店啊。邮包里是什么东西啊?"

"夫人,"邮差显得有些生气了,"我不知道。你干吗不下来把邮包领走,这样你不就知道里面是什么了嘛。"

"哦,我不可以那样做的。"妇女说。

"为什么呢?"邮差问。

"因为我不是史密斯夫人,"她说,"你走错了,史密斯夫人住在隔壁。"

---

expensive adj. 昂贵的;费钱的   find out 发现;查出

CULTURE SERIES

8

A Sad Story

Jim met two friends on the street. "Come back to my *apartment* for a meal," he said. "You can see the whole of the city from my bedroom window."

His two friends agreed and they went back with Jim to

伤心的故事

吉姆在街上遇见两个朋友。"到我的公寓去吃饭吧，"他说，"从我卧室的窗口可以俯瞰整座城市。"

两个朋友同意了，便和吉姆一起去他家。吉姆住在公寓的第四十层。

apartment　*n.*　公寓住宅　　　　　　　　　　agree　*v.*　赞同；同意

◆ A SAD STORY

the apartment building where he lived on the fortieth floor.

When they arrived, however, the *elevator* was *out of order*.

"I'm sorry," Jim said, "we'll have to walk."

"But it's forty floors!" his friends said.

"We'll talk as we climb," Jim said. "You can tell me the new *jokes* you've heard and when we get to my apartment I'll tell you a story."

His friends agreed and they started to climb the forty *flights* of stairs.

At last they reached the top floor and were standing outside the door of Jim's apartment.

"Now tell us a good story," his friends said.

Jim looked at them sadly and said, "Once upon a time there was a man who met two friends. He invited them to his apartment on the

---

可当他们到那儿时，电梯却坏了。

"不好意思，"吉姆说，"我们得步行上楼了。"

"可有四十层啊！"朋友说。

"咱们可以边说话边爬楼梯嘛。" 吉姆说，"你们可以给我讲些最近听到的笑话，咱们到楼上时，我再给你们讲个故事。"

朋友同意了，他们便开始爬四十层楼梯。

最后，他们到了顶层，站在吉姆家门外。

"现在轮到你给我们讲有趣的故事了！"朋友说。

吉姆伤心地看了他们一眼，说："从前，有个人遇见了两个朋友，便

---

elevator *n.* 电梯
joke *n.* 笑话；玩笑

out of order 坏了；失灵了
flight *n.* 一段楼梯

CULTURE SERIES

fortieth floor. The elevator wasn't *working* and they had to climb forty flights of stairs. When they reached the fortieth floor, he put his hand in his pocket for the key to the door of his apartment. It wasn't there. Then he remembered where it was. It was in his car."

邀请他们去第四十层的公寓吃饭。可电梯却坏了，因此他们不得不爬四十层的楼梯。当到达第四十层时，他把手伸进裤兜，想掏钥匙开门，可他突然记起不小心把钥匙忘在车上了。"

work　*v.* 运转顺利；进行顺利

◆ THE BEST SALESMAN IN THE WORLD

9

The Best Salesman In the World

Harry saw an *ad* in a window. It said: "Wanted. The Best Salesman in the World. *Top Pay*."

"I'm a great salesman," Harry told himself. "I can sell anything. I'll go in and ask for that job."

He went into the building and spoke to the *manager*.

世界上最优秀的推销员

哈瑞看到了橱窗内的一则广告,写着:"招聘:世界上最优秀的推销员,高薪。"

"我是很好的推销员,"哈瑞想,"我能把任何东西都销售出去,我得去应聘。"

于是他走进了那座大厦,对经理说:"我是世界上最优秀的推销员,把这份工作交给我吧。"

---

ad *n.* 广告
manager *n.* 经理

top pay 高薪

CULTURE SERIES

"I'm the best salesman in the world," he said. "Give me the job."

"You must *prove* you're the best," the manager said.

"I'll pass every test you give me," Harry told him.

"Good."

The manager took a box of candy out of his desk.

"Last week, I bought a thousand boxes of this candy. If you can sell them all before the end of the week, you can have the job."

"That's easy," Harry said.

He took the box of candy and left the office.

"那你得证明自己是最优秀的啊。"经理说。

"我肯定能通过你的每项测验。"哈瑞说。

"那好。"

经理从办公桌里拿出一盒糖。

"上周，我买了一千盒这种糖，如果在这周内你能把它们都推销出去，就可以得到这份工作。"

"那很容易啊！"哈瑞说。

他拿着糖离开了办公室。

---

prove *v.* 证明

◆ THE BEST SALESMAN IN THE WORLD

Every day and all day, he went from shop to shop, trying to sell boxes of the candy.

He couldn't sell one.

The candy was so bad he couldn't even *give* it *away*.

At the end of the week he went back to the manager.

"I'm sorry, sir," he said. "I was wrong about myself. I'm not the best salesman in the world, but I know who is."

"Oh," said the manager. "Who?"

"The person who sold you a thousand boxes of this candy," Harry said.

从这以后,他挨家店去推销糖。

但一盒也没卖出去。

因为糖的质量太差了,就连白送也没有人要。

到了周末,他回到经理那里。

"不好意思,先生,"他说,"我太高估自己了,我并不是世界上最优秀的推销员,但我知道谁是。"

"哦,"经理问,"谁啊?"

"就是那个卖给你一千盒糖果的人啊。"哈瑞说。

---

give away 赠送;赠给

CULTURE SERIES

10

Your Need Is Greater Then Mine

In many big cities there are people who cannot get work. Sometimes they do not want to work, but sometimes there isn't any work for them to do.

Some of these people *beg* for money. Some of them sell boxes of *matches* or cheap pens, and some of them sell flowers.

你比我更需要

在许多大城市里，有很多人没有工作。有的人不想工作，但有的人是找不到工作。

那些找不到工作的人便开始乞讨。有人卖火柴、有人卖便宜的笔、有人干脆卖花。

---

beg *v.* 乞讨　　　　　　　　　　　　　　　　　　　　match *n.* 火柴

◆ YOUR NEED IS GREATER THEN MINE

Andrew never gave money to *beggars*. "People should work for their money," he believed. He also believed there was work for everyone, which was not true.

One day when he was waiting for a bus, a beggar came up and asked him for money. The beggar was an old woman wearing very old and dirty clothes. She had no shoes and she was selling some *sweet-smelling* flowers.

"Give an old woman ten dollars, mister," she said to Andrew. "I haven't had a meal for three days."

"I'm not giving you ten dollars," Andrew said.

"What about five dollars then, mister?" the poor old woman asked. "That'll buy me a couple of pieces of bread."

安德鲁从来不施舍钱给乞丐。"人应该靠劳动赚钱，"他一直这样认为。他同样认为每个人都会有工作，但这种想法是不对的。

一天，在他等车时，有个乞丐走过来问他要钱。老太太穿得又脏又破，还没穿鞋，手里拿着带香味的鲜花叫卖着。

"先生，给老太太10美元吧。"她对安德鲁说，"我已经三天没有吃饭了。"

"我不会给你10美元的。" 安德鲁说。

"那5美元怎么样？"可怜的老太太问，"用这些钱可以买很多面包片。"

---

beggar *n.* 乞丐　　　　　　sweet-smelling *adj.* 芳香的；芬芳的

CULTURE SERIES

"No," Andrew said.

"Then what about one dollar?" the old woman asked. "I can buy an orange for one dollar."

"I haven't got one dollar," Andrew said. "Now go away."

The old woman looked at him *sadly*, and then gave him her flowers.

"Here, mister," she said. "You have these. You need them more than I do."

"不行,"安德鲁说。

"那1美元呢?"老太太问,"我可以买个橙子。"

"1美元我也没有,"安德鲁说,"你走吧。"

老人悲哀地看着他,把手里的鲜花递给了他。

"先生,拿去吧,"她说,"你比我更需要这些花。"

---

sadly *adv.* 伤心地;悲伤地

◆ A VERY IMPORTANT PERSON

11

A Very Important Person

Important people often like to show how important they are.

They usually have the largest cars. They live in the biggest houses. They wear the most expensive clothes. They eat in the best restaurants.

Mr Mammoth, the *president* of Acme Inc., was an important man. Acme

大人物

大人物通常喜欢炫耀自己有多重要。

他们一般都有最豪华的车，住最大的房子，穿最贵的衣服，去最好的餐厅吃饭。

阿克姆公司总裁猛马先生就是位重要人物。阿克姆公司也是这个国家

---

president　*n.*　总裁；总经理

CULTURE SERIES

Inc. was an important company, one of the biggest in the country. Thousands of men and women worked for it.

The offices of Acme Inc. were in The Acme Building. This was one of the tallest buildings in the city. It had fifty *floors*.

Mr Mammoth, the president, had his office on the top floor.

One day a man came to see him. He walked up to Mr Mammoth's *secretary*. She was, of course, the most beautiful secretary in the company.

"My name is John Watkins," he told her. "I have come to see Mr Mammoth. My *appointment* is at 10 o'clock."

The most beautiful secretary in the building looked at the clock on the wall. It was the largest clock in the company.

最大的公司之一，非常有地位。公司有几千名员工。

  阿克姆公司的办公楼在阿克姆大厦，是这座城市最高的楼之一，共50层。

  猛犸先生的办公室在最顶层。

  一天，有人来拜访猛犸先生。他走到猛犸先生的秘书面前——当然，秘书也是全公司最漂亮的。

  "我叫约翰·瓦特金斯，"他告诉她，"我是来拜访猛犸先生的，约会在10点。"

  这位最漂亮的秘书看了看墙上的钟——公司最大的钟。

---

floor *n.* （楼房的）层　　　　　　　　　　secretary *n.* 秘书
appointment *n.* 约会

◆ A VERY IMPORTANT PERSON

"It is 10 o'clock now," she said. "You are on time for your appointment. However, I am afraid you cannot see Mr Mammoth."

John Watkins was surprised.

"Oh? Why is that?" he asked.

"Mr Mammoth is playing *golf*."

"Oh," John Watkins said. "Then he won't be coming to his office today."

The most beautiful secretary in the company smiled at him.

"Mr Mammoth's already here," she said. "He has the largest office in the world."

"现在是10点,"她说,"你非常准时,但你恐怕见不着猛犸先生了。"

约翰·瓦特金斯非常惊奇。

"为什么呢?"他问。

"猛犸先生正在打高尔夫球。"

"哦,"约翰·瓦特金斯说,"那他今天不会来办公室了吧?"

最漂亮的秘书微笑地看着他。

"猛犸先生已经来了,"她说,"他的办公室是世界上最大的。"

---

golf *n.* 高尔夫球

CULTURE SERIES

12

Violin Lessons

"Daddy, can I learn to play the *violin*?" young Sarah asked her father. She was always asking for things and her father was not very pleased.

"You cost me a lot of money, Sarah," he said. "First you wanted to learn horseback riding, then dancing, then swimming. Now it's the violin."

"I'll play every day, Daddy," Sarah said. "I'll try very hard."

小提琴课程

"爸爸,我可以学拉小提琴吗?"小莎拉问爸爸。她总是给爸爸提很多要求,爸爸都不太乐意了。

"我已经在你身上花了很多钱了,莎拉,"他说,"你开始想学骑马,后来是舞蹈,再后来是游泳。现在又想学小提琴。"

"我会天天练习的,爸爸,"莎拉说,"我会非常用功的。"

---

violin *n.* 小提琴

◆ VIOLIN LESSONS

"All right," her father said. "This is what I'll do. I'll pay for you to have lessons for six weeks. At the end of six weeks you must play something for me. If you play well, you can have more lessons. If you play badly, I will stop the lessons."

"OK, Daddy," Sarah said. "That's fair."

He soon found a good violin teacher and Sarah began her lessons. The teacher was very expensive, but her father *kept his promise*.

The six weeks passed quickly. The time came for Sarah to play for her father.

She went to the living room and said, "I'm ready to play for you, Daddy."

"Fine, Sarah," her father said. "Begin."

"好吧，"爸爸说，"我让你学六周，然后你拉给我听。如果拉得好，我就让你接着学；如果不好的话，你就不能再学了。"

"好的，爸爸，"莎拉说，"这非常公平。"

他很快给莎拉找了一位非常优秀的小提琴教师，莎拉便开始学了。尽管学费非常贵，但爸爸还是履行了诺言。

六周很快就过去了，该莎拉给爸爸表演了。

她走进客厅对爸爸说："我已经准备好了，爸爸。"

"好的，莎拉，"父亲说，"开始吧。"

---

keep a promise 遵守诺言

CULTURE SERIES

She began to play. She played very badly. She made a *terrible noise*.

Her father had one of his friends with him, and the friend put his hands over his ears.

When Sarah finished, her father said, "Well done, Sarah. You can have more lessons."

Sarah ran happily out of the room. Her father's friend turned to him. "You've spent a lot of money, but she still plays very badly," he said.

"Well, that's true," her father said. "But since she started learning the violin, I've been able to buy five apartments in this building very cheaply. In another six weeks I'll own the whole building."

她开始演奏了，拉得非常糟糕，发出了刺耳的噪音。

爸爸请来的一个朋友都捂住了耳朵。

当莎拉结束时，父亲说："拉得很好，莎拉。你可以继续学习小提琴。"

莎拉高兴地跑出去了。他朋友转过身来，"你已经花了很多钱了，可她演奏得很糟糕啊，"他说。

"确实是。"父亲说，"但自从她学琴以来，我已经很便宜地买下了这座楼的五套房子。再过六周，整栋楼都会属于我了！"

---

terrible adj. 糟糕的；可怕的   noise n. 噪声；喧闹声

Not So Stupid

Two men were sitting together in an airplane. They were on a long *journey*.

One of the men was a teacher. The other was a farmer.

They sat without talking for a while, then the farmer said,

并不笨

飞机上有两个人邻座,他们都做长途旅行。

其中一人是教师,另一个是农夫。

有一阵子,他们都没说话。突然,农夫说:"我们做点什么来消磨时间吧。"

---

journey *n.* 旅行;旅程

CULTURE SERIES

"Let's do something to *pass the time*."

"What do you want to do?" the teacher asked.

"We can ask each other *riddles*," the farmer said. "You start."

"Let's make the *rules* first," the teacher said. "And let's make the game more interesting. Let's play it for money. If we don't know the answer to a riddle, we have to pay each other $100."

The farmer thought about this for a while. Then he said, "That's not fair. You are a teacher, an *educated* man. You know more things than I do. I am just a farmer."

"That's true," the teacher said. "What do you think we should do?"

"If you don't know the answer to a riddle, you pay me $100. If I don't know the answer to a riddle, I'll pay you $50."

"你想做什么呢？"教师问。

"咱们可以猜谜语。"农夫说，"你先出题。"

"那先定规则，"教师说，"咱们可以使游戏变得更有趣些——赌钱吧。如果我们之间谁要是猜不出谜底，就输给对方100美元。"

农夫想了一会，说："那不公平。你是教师，受过教育。你知道的肯定比我多。我只是一个农夫。"

"那倒是，"教师说，"那你说怎么办呢？"

"如果你不知道谜底，就付给我100美元；如果我不知道，只付给你

---

pass the time 消磨（时间）　　　　riddle n. 谜；谜语
rule n. 规则　　　　　　　　　　educated adj. 有教养的；受过教育的

◆ NOT SO STUPID

The teacher thought about this, then he said, "OK. That's fair. Who'll go first?"

"I will," the farmer said. "Here is my riddle. What has three legs when it walks, but only two legs when it flies?"

The teacher *repeated* the riddle. "What has three legs when it walks, but only two legs when it flies? Er,That's a good one. I'm afraid I don't know the answer."

He gave the farmer $100, then said, "Tell me the answer. What has three legs when it walks but only two legs when it flies?"

"I don't know," the farmer said, and gave him $50.

50美元。"

教师想了想，说："行，这样比较公平。谁先来？"

"我先来，"农夫说，"什么东西走路时三条腿，飞时两条腿？"

教师重复了谜语。"走时三条腿，飞时两条腿？非常好的谜语。我想我猜不出来。"

于是他给了农夫100美元，说，"告诉我谜底吧，什么东西走时三条腿，飞时两条腿？"

"我也不知道，"农夫说，然后给了教师50美元。

---

repeat *v.* 重复

CULTURE SERIES

14

No Elephants

Jill Jones got a new job in a different part of the city. She had to go to work every day by train.

There was only one other person on the train with her. He was a *well-dressed* man reading a newspaper.

没有大象

吉尔·琼斯在城市的另一头找到了一份工作。她每天必须坐火车去上班。火车上只有两个人。除了她还有一个衣着整洁的人正在读报。

well-dressed *adj.* 穿着考究的

◆ NO ELEPHANTS

Suddenly, about halfway through the *journey*, the man began *tearing* his newspaper into hundreds of small pieces.

Then he picked them up, opened the window and threw them all out.

This done, he sat down, closed his eyes, and slept for the rest of the journey.

The next day, Jill got on the same train. The same well-dressed man was there, reading a newspaper.

As before, about halfway through the journey, the man began tearing his newspaper into hundreds of small pieces. Then he picked the pieces up, opened the window and threw them all out.

This done, he sat down, closed his eyes, and slept for the rest of the journey.

This happened every day for a week.

坐到半道时，那人突然开始把报纸撕成了碎片。

然后他把碎片拾起来，打开窗户扔了出去。

接着，他坐下来，把眼睛闭上开始睡觉。

第二天，吉尔又乘坐同一列火车，那个衣着得体的人仍在读报。

就像上次那样，半道时，那人又开始把报纸撕成碎片，拾起来，打开窗户扔出去。

然后又坐下，闭上眼睛睡觉。

整整一周他都重复着这样的动作。

---

journey n. 旅程；旅行   tear v. 撕破；撕裂

CULTURE SERIES

At last, on Friday, Jill spoke to the man.

"Excuse me sir," she said, "I don't want to be *rude*, but I must ask you a question. When we are halfway through our journey, you tear your newspaper into hundreds of pieces and then throw them all out of the window. Please tell me, sir. Why do you do this?"

The well-dressed man smiled. "There's a *simple reason*," he said. "I like to sleep for part of the journey, but I cannot sleep if the train is full of elephants. So I throw the pieces of paper out to the elephants. It stops them from coming into the train."

"But there aren't any elephants on the train," Jill said.

"I know," the man said. "It works well, doesn't it?"

最后，周五那天，吉尔跟他攀谈起来。

"打扰了，先生，"她说，"我本不想如此鲁莽，但就想问个明白。为何你每天半道时就撕碎报纸，然后扔到窗外，能告诉我原因吗？先生。"

衣着整洁的绅士笑了笑。"原因非常简单，"他说，"我想在接下来的旅途中睡上一觉，如果火车里都是大象的话，我睡不着。于是我就把报纸屑扔出窗外，这样大象就不会上火车了。"

"但火车上并没有大象啊！"吉尔说。

"我知道啊，"他说，"这不正说明我的做法奏效了吗？"

---

rude *adj.* 无礼的；粗野的
reason *n.* 原因；理由

simple *adj.* 简单的；简易的

How Wars Begin

The Stevenson family was having dinner. The family ate without talking for several minutes, then Tom said, "Daddy, do you know how *wars* begin?"

Mr Stevenson thought for a *moment*, then he said, "Yes, I think so. I'll give you an example. We'll take two countries, Britain and the United States. If Britain fought

战争是怎样开始的

史蒂文森家人正在吃晚餐。沉默了好几分钟后,汤姆突然问:"爸爸,你知道战争是怎样开始的吗?"

史蒂文森先生想了想,说:"我知道。给你举个例子,英国和美国。如果英国和美国打仗……"

war n. 战争　　　　　　　　　　　　moment n. 瞬间

CULTURE SERIES

with the United States..."

Mrs Stevenson laughed. "That's *crazy*," she said to her husband. "Britain and the United States have been friends for over two hundred years. They'll never fight."

"Yes, I know that," Mr Stevenson said. "I was only using them as an example."

"But they're not a good example," Mrs Stevenson said. "France and Germany are a better example."

"Britain and the United States are the best example," Mr Stevenson *replied*. "They are friends now but they were *enemies* in the past. They fought a war!"

"But that was a long time ago," Mrs Stevenson said. "You should use more *modern* examples."

史蒂文森夫人笑了。"那太傻了,"她对丈夫说,"英国和美国已经和好两百多年了,它们不可能打仗啊。"

"是,我知道,"史蒂文森先生说,"我只是举个例子而已。"

"可这并不是个好例子啊,"史蒂文森夫人说,"法国和德国的例子就比这个例子好。"

"英国和美国是最好的例子,"史蒂文森先生回答说,"它们现在是朋友,可过去是敌人。他们发动了战争!"

"但那是很久以前的事了,"史蒂文森夫人说,"你应该举些更现代一点的例子。"

---

crazy *adj.* 发疯的;糊涂的
enemy *n.* 仇敌;敌人

reply *v.* 回答
modern *adj.* 现代的

◆ HOW WARS BEGIN

"And you should let me answer my son's question," Mr Stevenson said angrily.

"Not when you give him wrong answers," Mrs Stevenson said.

"I am not giving him wrong answers!" Mr Stevenson *shouted*. "I am giving him *perfectly* good answers."

"Don't shout at me!" Mrs Stevenson cried. "I'm not one of your stupid friends."

"My friends aren't stupid!" Mr Stevenson stood up and walked angrily out the room.

"Now I'll answer your question," Mrs Stevenson said to her son.

"It's all right, Mom," he said. "You and Dad already have."

"你应该让我回答儿子的问题。"史蒂文森先生生气地说。

"但并不是要你给他错误的答案啊。"史蒂文森夫人说。

"我没给他错误的答案!"史蒂文森喊道,"我给他的答案非常恰当。"

"别冲我大喊大叫的!" 史蒂文森夫人哭了,"我可不是你那些愚蠢的朋友。"

"我的朋友才不愚蠢呢!"史蒂文森先生站起来,非常生气地走出了房间。

"现在我可以回答你的问题了," 史蒂文森夫人对她儿子说。

"是的,妈妈," 他说,"你和爸爸的战争已经开始了。"

---

shout *v.* 呼喊;喊叫   perfectly *adv.* 十分;完全地

16

The Diet

Mrs Stewart was worried about her weight.

"I'm much too fat," she told her friend. "I need to lose a lot of weight but I don't know how to do it."

"Go and see Doctor Coffey," her friend said. "He'll tell you how to

---

节食

斯图尔特夫人十分担心自己的体重。

她向朋友诉苦:"我太胖了,必须减肥,可又不知道如何减,怎么办啊!"

朋友建议她:"去问问高菲医生吧,他会给你些建议的。"

◆ THE DIET

lose weight."

Mrs Stewart visited Doctor Coffey and told him her problem.

"It isn't difficult to lose weight," he told her. "All you need to do is go on a *diet*. I'll give you one."

He began to write on a piece of paper.

"Eat lots of fruit and vegetables. Also eat a lot of *lean* meat and *grains*."

When he finished, he handed her the piece of paper.

"Here you are," he said. "Eat all those things and you'll soon lose weight."

A few weeks later, Mrs Stewart's friend called on her.

She was surprised to see that she was even fatter than before and that she was eating a *huge* sandwich with chocolate cake and

---

斯图尔特夫人去拜访了高菲医生，并向他倾诉了自己的烦恼。

医生说："减肥并不难啊，你只要注意节食就好了，我会给你提供一份健康饮食的食谱。"

医生边说边在纸上写着："多吃蔬菜和水果，多吃瘦肉和五谷杂粮。"

写完后，医生把那张纸递给她。

"按照这个做，你很快就会瘦下来的。"

几周后，斯图尔特夫人的朋友来看她。

她正在吃冰激凌和一个巨型巧克力三明治，比以前更胖了，她的朋友

---

diet n. 节食；控制饮食
grain n. 谷物

lean adj. 瘦的
huge adj. 非常大的；巨大的

CULTURE SERIES

ice cream.

"I thought you *were on a diet*," she said.

"Oh, I am," Mrs Stewart replied. "I've already had all the food on my diet today. Now I'm eating my dinner."

惊呆了。

"我还以为你会按照食谱合理饮食呢，"她朋友说。

斯图尔特夫人回答说："对啊，我正是遵照食谱做的。今天我已经把食谱上列的所有食物都吃了，现在正吃晚餐呢。"

---

be on a diet 节食；控制饮食

A Holiday From School

Tommy hated school and was always looking for excuses not to go.

If he *sneezed*, he asked his mother to write a note saying he had a cold.

If he had a *headache*, he asked his mother to take him to the doctor during school hours.

He spent more time at home than he did at school.

On the days that he did go to school, he looked for excuses to

逃学

汤姆不愿意去上学，总找借口逃学。

他若打喷嚏，就央求妈妈写张纸条给老师说他感冒了。

他若头痛，就嚷嚷着不去上学了，要妈妈带他去看病。

他在家里的时间比在学校的时间多得多。

他就是去上学，也总找借口提前回来。

---

sneeze *v.* 打喷嚏   headache *n.* 头痛

CULTURE SERIES

come home early.

One day he came home from school in the *middle* of the morning. His father was surprised.

"You're home early," he said. "Is school closed today?"

"No, Dad," Tommy said. "It's open. I came home early."

"How did you do that?" his father asked him. "What did you say to the teacher?"

"I told her that I had a new baby brother and that I had to come home and help you."

"But your mother has had *twins*," his father said, "a boy and a girl. You've got a baby brother and a baby sister."

"Yes, I know, Dad," Tommy said. "I'm *saving up* my baby sister for next week."

一天,上午刚过去一半,他就从学校跑回家了。

爸爸感到很奇怪,就问:"你怎么这么早就回来了?学校今天不上课吗?"

"不是的,爸爸,学校当然上课了,我提前回来的。"汤姆回答。

爸爸问他:"你回来这么早,怎么向老师请假的?"

汤姆说:"我跟老师说,我小弟弟刚出生,所以必须回家帮您啊。"

"但你妈妈生的是龙凤胎啊,你既有一个小弟弟,还有一个小妹妹呢。"爸爸说。

汤姆回答:"是的,我知道,爸爸,我把小妹妹留到下周再用。"

---

middle n. 中间;当中
save up 储存;备用

twin n. 双胞胎之一

Love Letters

Jenny Gordon was a very kind and beautiful woman and before she *got married*, many men were in love with her.

Many of them wrote to her, telling her how *wonderful* she was, how much they loved her and wanted to marry her.

情书

贞妮·戈登非常美丽、善良。结婚前，许多男人都深爱着她。

有许多人给她写信，称赞她有多么出众，他们有多么爱她，想娶她为妻。

---

wonderful *adj.* 极好的，绝妙的　　　　　　get married 结婚

CULTURE SERIES

Jenny kept all these letters. She *tied* them up with a red *ribbon* and put them away in an old box.

She never looked at them as she was happily married; however, they were a part of her life and she did not want to throw them away.

Jenny had a daughter, Sue. Sue was six.

One day, Jenny had to leave Sue alone for half an hour.

"Now be a good girl," she said. "Play quietly. If you need anything, go to the lady next door."

When she *returned* home, she asked Sue, "Have you been a good girl?"

贞妮把所有的信都保留了下来，还用红色的丝带将这些信系好，保存在一个旧盒子里。

她的婚姻很幸福，因此她再也没看过这些信。然而，这些信却成为她生活的一部分，她不想把它们丢掉。

贞妮有一个6岁的女儿，名字叫苏。

一天，贞妮有事要外出半个小时，因此不得不把苏一个人留在家里。

她说："乖女儿，在家里好好玩，别吵着邻居。你要是有什么需要，就去找隔壁的阿姨。"

她回来后问苏："你在家里乖不乖啊？"

---

tie *v.* 捆；系　　　　　　　　　　　　　　　　　ribbon *n.* 缎带
return *v.* 回；返回

◆ LOVE LETTERS

"Oh, yes, Mommy," Sue said.

"What did you do while I was out?" Jenny asked her.

"I played mailman," Sue told her.

"How could you play mailman, darling?" Sue asked. "You didn't have any letters."

"Oh, yes I did, Mommy," Sue said. "I found some in an old box *upstairs*. They were tied up with a red ribbon. I put one in every mailbox on the street. Wasn't I a good girl?"

"哦，是的，妈妈，我很乖，"苏答道。

"我出去的这段时间你都做什么了？"贞妮问女儿。

苏告诉妈妈："我当了回邮递员。"

贞妮问道："宝贝，你怎么当邮递员的啊？你没有信可以送啊。"

"哦，不，妈妈，我有信送啊。在楼上我发现了一个旧盒子，里面装着一些用红色丝带系好的信。我在这条街上每家的信箱里都投了一封。我是不是很乖啊？"

upstairs *adv.* 在楼上

CULTURE SERIES

19

Quick Service

A man took a pair of shoes to a shoe *repair* shop and said to the *shoemaker*, "I'd like you to repair these shoes for me, please."

"Certainly, sir," the shoemaker said.

"When will they be ready?" the man asked.

"I'm a bit busy, but they'll probably be ready for you on Thursday," he said.

高效率的服务

一个男人拿了一双鞋到修鞋店去修，他对鞋匠说："请帮我修一下这双鞋好吗？"

"当然可以，先生，"鞋匠说。

他问鞋匠："哪天可以修好？"

"现在有点忙，但周四应该就能修好，到时候你过来取就行了。"鞋匠说。

---

repair *n.* 修理；修补　　　　　　　　　　　　shoemaker *n.* 鞋匠

◆ QUICK SERVICE

"That's fine," the man said.

The next morning he received a letter *offering* him a job in another country. Within 24 hours he was on an airplane to his new job.

Twenty years passed and he returned to his hometown.

He remembered his shoes.

"They were a good pair of shoes," he thought. "I *wonder* if the shoemaker is still there and still has them. I'll go and see."

He was pleased to see that the shoemaker was still in the same shop, although he was an old man by now.

"Good morning," he said to him. "Twenty years ago, I brought in a pair of shoes to be repaired. Do you think you've still got them?"

"好的。"

第二天上午,他收到一封聘书,聘请他去另外一个国家工作。仅一天之内,他就飞到了另一个国度,开始了一份新的工作。

20年过去了,他回到了家乡。

突然想起了那双鞋。

他思忖道:"那还是一双好鞋呢,不知道那家修鞋店还在不在?那双鞋还在不在?我要去看看。"

他欣喜地看到,鞋匠还在那家修鞋店里,只是已经苍老了许多。

他走上去跟鞋匠打招呼:"早上好!20年前我曾带了一双鞋过来

---

offer *v.* 提供　　　　　　　　　　wonder *v.* 好奇;想知道

CULTURE SERIES

"Name?" the old shoemaker asked.

"Smith," the man said.

"I'll go and see. They may be out back."

The shoemaker went out to the back of his shop and a few minutes later returned, carrying the pair of shoes.

"Here we are," he said. "One pair of brown shoes to be repaired. I'm a bit busy now, but they'll *probably* be ready on Thursday."

修，那双鞋还在吗？"

  这位老鞋匠询问了他的姓名。

  他回答说叫史密斯。

  鞋匠说："我去看看，可能在后院。"

  鞋匠走到店铺的后院，几分钟后，拎了一双鞋回来了。

  鞋匠说："哦，找到了，是一双要修理的棕色皮鞋。可我现在有点忙，但周四应该就能修好。"

---

probably *adv.* 很可能；大概

20

The Umbrella Man

One day, Jack's wife was cleaning out a *closet*.

"Look at all these *umbrellas*," Jack's wife said to him. "There are eight and they are all *broken*."

"I'll take them all to the umbrella shop and have them repaired," Jack said. "They are too good to *throw away*."

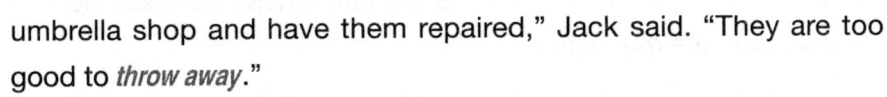

Jack took the eight umbrellas to the shop and left them there.

偷伞的人

一天，杰克的妻子正在打扫壁橱。

妻子说："看看这些伞吧，八把伞，都坏了。"

杰克说："我把这些伞拿到雨伞修理铺去修修。伞都很贵，丢了太可惜啊。"

于是杰克把这八把伞留在了店铺。店员说第二天就可以修好。

---

closet *n.* 壁橱
broken *adj.* 损坏的；出故障的

umbrella *n.* 雨伞
throw away 丢弃某物

CULTURE SERIES

"They'll be ready tomorrow," the shopkeeper said.

That evening Jack went home from the office by bus, as usual.

He sat next to an old woman. She had an umbrella on the floor near her.

When the bus reached his stop, he picked up her umbrella and stood up.

"Hey!" the woman said. "That's my umbrella."

"I'm so sorry," Jack said, giving it to her. "I wasn't thinking. Please *forgive* me."

The next day he *collected* the umbrellas from the umbrella shop and got on the bus.

As he sat down, a voice behind him said, "You have certainly had a *successful* day!"

He turned around and saw the woman whose umbrella he had almost taken the day before.

当天晚上，杰克如同往常那样坐公共汽车下班回家。

他旁边坐着一位老太太。老太太的伞就放在旁边地上。

汽车到站时，他捡起老太太的那把伞站了起来。

老太太急了，喊道，"嗨，那是我的伞。"

杰克把伞还给她，抱歉地说："对不起，我刚才走神了，请您原谅我。"

第二天，他去伞铺取完伞后，上了公共汽车。

他找了个位置坐下来，突然身后有人说："你今天的收获不小啊！"

他向四周望了望，原来是昨天差点错拿了她伞的那位老太太。

---

forgive *v.* 原谅
successful *adj.* 获得成功的；取得成效的

collect *v.* 接走；领取；收取

◆ FISHING CAN BE DANGEROUS

Fishing Can Be Dangerous

Old Peter liked fishing. Whenever he had any free time he drove into the countryside, found a good place to fish, and spent a few hours fishing.

The problem was that most of the best places to fish were on *private* land, and Peter often had to pull his *rod* out of

钓鱼的麻烦

彼得很喜欢钓鱼。一有时间，他就开车到乡下，找个好地方，钓几个小时的鱼。

可钓鱼的最佳场所大部分都归私人所有。只要主人一来，彼得就急忙将鱼竿从水中拽起，匆忙逃跑。

---

private *adj.* 私人的　　　　　　　　　　rod *n.* 棒；竿

CULTURE SERIES

the water quickly and run off with it when the owner of the land *came along*.

One day he was sitting by a river that ran through a rich man's *property* when he fell asleep.

He was *awakened* by a voice saying, "You'll never catch anything using that *bait*."

Peter looked up and saw a man standing behind him.

"What do you mean?" Peter said. "There's nothing wrong with this bait. I always use it. I've caught thirty fish with it today already."

"How very interesting," the man said. "Do you know who I am?"

Peter shook his head.

"I'm the owner of this land."

一天，他坐在河边钓鱼，这条河刚巧穿过一富人家的私人宅地，钓着钓着，不一会就睡着了。

突然有个声音把他惊醒："用那样的鱼饵，你什么鱼也钓不上来。"

彼得抬起头，一个男人站在身后。

彼得说："你什么意思？鱼饵没有问题。我总用这种鱼饵，都有收获的。我今天已经钓了30条鱼了。"

"真有趣，你知道我是谁吗？"男人说。

彼得摇了摇头。

"我是这块地的主人。"

---

come along 到达；出现
awaken *v.* 醒；弄醒

property *n.* 房地产；所有物
bait *n.* 诱饵

◆ FISHING CAN BE DANGEROUS

Peter thought very quickly.

"Do you know who I am?" he asked.

The man shook his head.

"I'm the biggest *liar* in the country," Peter told him.

And with this he pulled his *line* out of the water and ran off as fast as he could.

彼得灵机一动，问道："你知道我是谁吗？"

那个男人摇了摇头。

彼得说："我是村里最善于说谎的人。"

说完，他急忙将鱼线从水中拽出，逃之夭夭了。

---

liar *n.* 说谎者 　　　　　　　　　　　　　　　　　　line *n.* 线

CULTURE SERIES

22

The Earthquake

Johnny lived with his mother and father in a small town in the mountains.

One day there was an *earthquake* near the town. Many houses were *damaged*. Everyone thought that there would soon be another earthquake.

They were worried that the second

地震

约翰尼和父母住在山区的一个小镇里。

一天，小镇附近发生了地震，许多房屋都被摧毁，所有人都认为还会有一次地震。

人们担心第二次地震会比第一次更糟。

---

earthquake *n.* 地震   damage *v.* 毁坏；破坏

◆ THE EARTHQUAKE

earthquake would be worse than the first.

"We must send Johnny to a *safe* place," Johnny's mother said to her husband. "Many of our friends are sending their children to *relatives* in other towns."

"We'll send him to my brother, Peter," Johnny's father said. "He lives a long way away. Johnny will be safe with him."

He telephoned Johnny's Uncle Peter and asked him if he would let Johnny live with him.

"He's a good boy," he said. "He won't give you any trouble."

"All right," Johnny's Uncle Peter said, "but I'm not used to children. I live a very quiet and *peaceful* life."

"You won't know Johnny's in the house," his father told him.

约翰尼的母亲和丈夫商量,"我们必须把约翰尼送到安全的地方。有许多朋友都把孩子送到其他镇上的亲戚家了。"

约翰尼的父亲说:"我们把孩子送到哥哥彼得家吧。他住的地方离这里比较远,约翰尼住在那里会很安全的。"

父亲给约翰尼的叔叔彼得打了个电话,问他能否让约翰尼去。

父亲说:"约翰尼是个好孩子,他不会给你添麻烦的。"

彼得说:"好的,但我不习惯和孩子住在一起。我喜欢安静的生活。"

"你都不会感觉到约翰在你家的,"父亲说。

---

safe *adj.* 无危险的;安全的   relative *n.* 亲戚;亲属
peaceful *adj.* 安静的;安宁的

CULTURE SERIES

So Johnny, who was five, went to live with his uncle.

Two days later, his mother and father *received* a *telegram* from Peter.

It said: "Am returning child. Please send earthquake."

因此，5岁的约翰尼就去和叔叔一块住了。

两天后，父母收到彼得的电报。

上面写道："欲归还孩子，请将地震发过来。"

---

receive *v.* 收到；得到　　　　　　　　　　　　　　telegram *n.* 电报

A Family Secret

Arnold Johnson was a *proud* man. "I am sure my family is one of the oldest in the country," he often told people. "It has a long history."

One day he went to see an *expert* in family history, Mrs Green.

家族秘密

阿诺德·约翰逊是一个非常傲慢的人。

他经常说:"我相信我的家族是整个国家最古老的家族之一,有很久远的家族史。"

一天,他去拜访家族史方面的专家格林夫人。

---

proud *adj.* 自豪的;引以为荣的   expert *n.* 专家;能手

CULTURE SERIES

"I want you to find out everything about my family," he said. "Where do we come from? Who was the first Johnson? Were there any famous people in the family? Do I have any rich relatives?"

"OK," Mrs Green said, "but it will cost you $2,000."

Arnold thought about this. Two thousand dollars was a lot of money.

At last he said, "All right. But for $2,000 I want a *complete* history. I want full *details*."

The expert agreed. "Come back in three months," she said.

Three months later Arnold visited Mrs Green again.

"Well," he said, "have you found out everything about my family?"

他说:"我希望你能查一查有关我家族的事。我们是从什么地方来的?约翰逊家族中的第一个人是谁?家族中有名人吗?我有富有的亲属吗?"

格林夫人说:"可以,但你要交2000美元。"

阿诺德想了想,2000美元是一大笔钱呢。

最后他说:"好吧。2000美元可以,但得你把整个家族的细枝末节都查清楚。"

专家同意了,让他3个月后回来。

3个月后,阿诺德再次来拜访格林夫人。

他说:"请问我家族的一切你都查清楚了吗?"

---

complete *adj.* 全部的;完整的   detail *n.* 细节;详情

◆ A FAMILY SECRET

"Yes," she said. "It is a very interesting family. However, my price is now $5,000."

"Five thousand dollars!" Arnold shouted. "But you told me the cost was only $2,000."

"I know. It was $2,000 to find out about your family," she said. "It is another $3,000 to keep what I found out *secret*!"

"是的,你的家族非常有趣。但是,现在你得交5000美元,"她说。

阿诺德惊叫道:"5000美元!你告诉我只要2000美元啊!"

她慢条斯理地说:"是的,我知道,2000美元是调查你家族史的辛苦费,另外3000美元是信息保密费。"

---

secret *n.* 秘密

CULTURE SERIES

24

No Point

Two days after Simon's fifth birthday, he went to school for the first time.

His mother bought him new clothes, and a *special* bag to carry his pens and books in.

The school was a long way from

没意思

西蒙过完5岁生日后的第三天,他要上学了。

妈妈给他买了件新衣服,还特地给他买了个书包,用来装书和钢笔。

学校离家很远,所以一大早妈妈就把他送到学校大门口。

---

special adj. 特殊的;特别的

◆ NO POINT

his home, so Simon's mother took him to school in the morning, and left him at the school *gate*.

"Enjoy yourself, Simon," she said, "and be good. The teacher will tell me if you're not."

Then she left him and went back home. At half past three she went back to the school to pick him up. She waited outside with many other mothers. Soon he came out and ran up to her.

"Did you enjoy your first day at school?" she asked him.

He shook his head.

"No," he said, "and I'm never going back there again."

His mother was very surprised.

　　妈妈嘱咐他:"祝你愉快,西蒙。在学校里要听老师的话,如果你不听话,老师会告诉我的!"

　　说完就转身回家了。下午3:30分,她回学校接西蒙。像其他母亲一样,她一直在外面等着。很快西蒙就出来了,向妈妈跑了过来。

　　"第一天上学高兴吗?"妈妈问他。

　　西蒙摇了摇头。

　　他说:"不高兴,我再也不想上学了。"

　　妈妈非常吃惊。

---

gate *n.* 门;大门

CULTURE SERIES

"What's the matter?" she asked him. "Has someone been *unkind* to you?"

"No," he replied.

"Did you miss me?" his mother asked him. "Is that why you don't want to go to school again?"

"No," he replied.

"Then tell me the reason," his mother said.

"All right. I can't read. I can't write. I can't *spell*. I can't do *math* and the teacher won't let me talk. What's the *point* of going to school when I can't do anything there?"

她问："怎么了，有人对你不友好吗？"

"没有，"西蒙回答。

妈妈问他："你想妈妈了？是因为这你才不想回去上学的吗？"

"不是，"他回答。

"那是什么原因啊？"妈妈说。

"我不会看书，不会写字，不会拼写，不会算术，老师还不让我说话，我什么都不能做，上学还有什么意思啊？"

---

unkind *adj.* 残酷的；不友好的
math *n.* 数学

spell *v.* 拼写
point *n.* 原因；理由

◆ LONG LIFE

25

Long Life

A man was selling *medicines* at a *fair*. At first he sold bottles of a *cure* for colds just a dollar a bottle.

Many people wanted to buy it and the man's young *assistant* moved quickly through the crowd collecting money and handing out bottles of the cold cure.

长寿

一个人在集市上卖感冒药。一开始，他一瓶只卖一美元。

许多人争先恐后地要买他的感冒药。年轻的女助手麻利地在人群中穿梭，边收钱边向人群分发药品。

---

medicine *n.* 药；药水
cure *n.* 疗程；疗法

fair *n.* （买卖农副产品和牲畜的）集市
assistant *n.* 助手；助理

CULTURE SERIES

Then, when he had a big crowd, the man held up a very small bottle. "And now, ladies and gentlemen," he shouted, "here is the medicine you have been waiting for. The cure for old age. Drink just one bottle of this and you will live forever."

"And, ladies and gentlemen," the man continued, "I'm not going to *charge* you a hundred dollars a bottle for this wonderful medicine. I'm not going to charge you fifty dollars a bottle. I'm not going to charge you twenty-five dollars a bottle. No, ladies and gentlemen, I'm going to charge you just ten dollars a bottle. Think, my friends, for ten dollars you can live forever."

Most of the people in the crowd did not *believe* this.

后来，人越聚越多，他举起一个非常小的瓶子，向人群大喊："女士们、先生们，这是你们一直以来梦寐以求的抗衰老的药。只喝一瓶，你就可以长寿！"

他继续喊道："女士们、先生们，这种灵丹妙药，我不会卖你们100美元或50美元一瓶，也不会卖你们25美元一瓶的。女士们、先生们，我只卖你们10美元一瓶！想一想，朋友们，只需花10美元，你就可以长寿！"

人群中，大部分人都不相信他的话。

charge v. 要价；收费　　　　　　　　　　　believe v. 相信

◆ LONG LIFE

One person shouted, "If it will make you live forever, why don't you drink it?"

Then another person cried, "Yes, you look as if you're at least sixty years old."

"Thank you, sir, thank you," the man replied, "I'm so *glad* you said that. My real age is three hundred twenty-nine."

The crowd laughed at this but there were still a few people who wanted to believe the man. One of them spoke to the man's assistant as she *passed by*. "Is that true," he asked, "that he's three hundred twenty-nine?"

"Don't ask me," the assistant said, "I've only worked for him for a hundred fifty years."

一个人喊道:"如果这药能使你长寿的话,你怎么不喝呢?"

接着又有人喊道:"对啊,你看起来至少有60岁了。"

卖药的人答道:"谢谢你,先生,谢谢。你这么说我很高兴。我的真实年龄是329岁。"

人们哄笑起来,但仍有几个人相信他的话。有个人问从身旁经过的助手,"是真的吗?他真的是329岁?"

助手说:"别问我,我才为他工作了150年而已。"

---

glad *adj.* 高兴的;感激的   pass by 经过

The Bank Robber

A bank was robbed by an *armed* robber.

He walked into the bank, went up to the bank *teller*, *pointed* a gun at her and said, "Give me all the money or I'll *shoot*."

The bank teller was frightened and did as the robber asked.

银行劫匪

一家银行遭到持枪歹徒的抢劫。

他走进银行，径直走向银行出纳员，用枪指着她说，"把所有的钱都交出来，否则我毙了你。"

银行出纳员吓坏了，遵照劫匪的要求做了。

---

armed *adj.* 武装的；装甲的
point *v.* 用（某物）瞄准（人或物）
teller *n.* （银行的）出纳员
shoot *v.* 开枪

♦ THE BANK ROBBER

The police later asked the bank teller if she could tell them anything about the robber.

"He wore a *stocking* over his face," the bank teller said. "I'm afraid I can't tell you what he looked like."

A week later, the bank was robbed again.

"I'm sure it was the same man," the bank teller said. "I didn't see his face, because he had a stocking over it again, but the voice was the same when he said, 'Give me all the money or I'll shoot.'"

A week later, the bank was robbed for the third time.

"Was it the same man?" the police asked the bank teller.

"Oh, yes, I'm sure it was," the bank teller said. "I didn't see his face because he wore a stocking over it again, but it was the same voice."

后来警察问出纳员是否能描述出劫匪的特征。

出纳员说："他脸上蒙着丝袜，恐怕我无法描述他的面部特征。"

一周之后，这家银行又遭抢劫了。

出纳员说："我确信是同一个人。可我没看清他的脸，因为他这一次还是蒙着丝袜。但是，当他说，'把所有的钱都交出来，否则我毙了你'的时候，我能听出是同一个人的声音。"

又过了一周，银行又遭抢劫了。

警察问出纳员，"是同一个人做的吗？"

出纳员说："哦，是的，我确信是同一个人。我没看清他的脸，因为

---

stocking *n.* （女用）长筒袜

CULTURE SERIES

"Are you sure you didn't *notice* anything else about the man?" the police asked. "A little detail. Anything that might help us find him."

The bank teller thought for a minute, then she said, "There is one thing."

"And what is that?" the police said hopefully.

"Every time he comes in and *robs* us," the teller said, "he's better dressed than before."

他仍然蒙着丝袜，但听声音是同一个人。"

警察问："你确定没有注意到任何其他有关这人的细节吗？哪怕一点蛛丝马迹，任何事情都可能对我们的破案有帮助。"

出纳员想了一会，说："哦，有一件事。"

"什么事？"警察满怀希望地问。

出纳员说："每次他来抢劫，都比前一次穿得更好了。"

---

notice *v.* 注意到；看到　　　　　　　　　　　　　　　　rob *v.* 抢劫

The Big Baby

"You'll have to take care of the baby today," a woman told her husband. "I'm not feeling well."

"Then you must stay in bed and rest, dear," her husband said. "I'll be pleased to look after our baby."

"Thank you. I'll have a quiet day

大婴儿

妻子对丈夫说:"今天你得照顾宝宝,因为我感觉不舒服。"

"那你就躺在床上休息吧,亲爱的,我很乐意照顾宝宝。"丈夫说。

妻子对他说:"谢谢你,亲爱的,我终于可以安静一天了,很快我就会好的。"

CULTURE SERIES

and I'll soon get better," his wife told him.

"Shall I go shopping for you as well?" her husband asked.

She was very pleased and said, "That will help me a lot. I'll give you a list of things to buy."

She wrote out the list and gave it to him.

"You can get all these things at the *supermarket*," she said. "You can put the baby in the shopping *cart*, so you won't have to leave him outside."

The man took the baby to the supermarket and put him in the shopping cart. Then he pushed the shopping cart along the *rows* of things to buy and looked for those that were on his list.

丈夫说："我也可以替你去购物。"

妻子非常高兴，说道："亲爱的，你可帮我大忙了。我给你列个购物单。"

她列了需要买的东西，把单子递给丈夫。

"你可以在超市买到这些东西。到时你可以把婴儿放在购物的手推车里，这样就不至于把宝宝留在外面了。" 她告诉丈夫。

丈夫把婴儿带到超市，把他放在购物的手推车里。然后，他把手推车推到购物架旁，开始挑选单子上所列的商品。

---

supermarket *n.* 超级市场　　　　　　　　　　cart *n.* 手推车；马车
row *n.* （人或物的）一排；一行

◆ THE BIG BABY

At first all was well, but then the baby began to cry.

Then he started to *scream*.

And scream!

And SCREAM!

"Keep *calm*, George," the man said. "Don't get excited. Don't shout, George. Don't lose your temper, George."

A woman in the supermarket heard him saying these things. She walked up to him.

"I think you are wonderful," she said. "You are so *patient* with your little George."

"Madam," the man said, "I'm George. He's Edward."

一开始，一切都很正常，但后来，婴儿哭起来。紧接着，哇哇大哭，声音越来越大，似乎要喊破喉咙。

"镇定点，乔治。不要生气，不要发脾气，不要失态。"

超市里一个女人听到他的话，朝他走过来。

她夸奖说："你简直太棒了，对你的小乔治这么有耐心。"

"夫人，我才是乔治呢，他叫艾德华，"丈夫说。

---

scream *v.* 尖声喊叫；惊呼   calm *adj.* 镇静的；心平气和的
patient *adj.* 耐心的

CULTURE SERIES

28

In the Air

Matt and his wife lived in the country. Matt was very *stingy* and hated spending money. One day a fair came to the nearby town.

"Let's go to the fair, Matt," his wife said. "We haven't been anywhere for a long time."

Matt thought about this for a while.

坐飞机

马特和妻子住在乡下。马特非常吝啬，极其讨厌花钱。一天，附近的城镇举办一次集会。

妻子说："亲爱的，我们去集市吧。我们已经很久没有到处逛逛了。"

马特想了一会儿，琢磨着去集市就得花钱。最后他开口说："好吧，

---

stingy *adj.* 吝啬的；小气的

◆ IN THE AIR

He knew he would have to spend money at the fair. At last he said, "All right, but I'm not going to spend much money. We'll look at things, but we won't buy anything."

They went to the fair and looked at all the things to buy. There were many things Matt's wife wanted to buy, but he would not let her spend any money.

Then, in a nearby *field*, they saw a small airplane.

"Fun *flights*!" the notice said, "10 dollars for 10 minutes."

Matt had never been in an airplane and he wanted to go on a fun flight. However, he didn't want to have to pay for his wife, as well.

"I've only got $10," he told the *pilot*. "Can my wife come with me

---

但是我不想花太多的钱。我们只看，不买。"

他们去了集市，看到了好多想买的东西。妻子想买，但是马特却不让她花一分钱。

后来，他们看到一架小型飞机停在附近的一块空地上。

海报上写着："想体会在天上飞的乐趣吗？10分钟10美元。"

马特从未坐过飞机，想体会一下在天上飞的乐趣。然而，他却不想为妻子花钱。

他问飞行员："我只有10美元，我的妻子可以随我免费乘坐吗？"

---

field *n.* 田；地
pilot *n.* 飞行员；飞机驾驶员

flight *n.* 飞翔；飞行

CULTURE SERIES

for free?" The pilot wasn't selling many tickets, so he said, "I'll make a *bargain* with you. If your wife doesn't scream or shout, she can have a free flight."

Matt agreed, and got into the small airplane with his wife.

The pilot took off and made his airplane do all kinds of things. At one moment it was flying *upside down*.

When the plane landed, the pilot said, "OK. Your wife didn't make a sound. She can have her ride free."

"Thank you," Matt said. "It wasn't easy for her, you know, especially when she fell out."

飞行员并没有卖出去几张票，因此他说："我可以给你打折，只要你妻子不尖叫，不大喊，就可以免费。"

马特同意了，就和妻子一同登上了那架小型飞机。

飞机起飞了，还在天上做了各式各样的动作。有一刻，飞机还在空中垂直向下降落。

飞机着陆时，飞行员说："很好，你的妻子没发出一点声音，她可以免费。"

马特说："谢谢。要知道，对她来说可真不容易，特别是当她从飞机上掉下去的时候。"

---

bargain *n.* 交易；协议   upside down 倒转地

On Guard

Two *unemployed* men, Len and Ted, were sitting in a restaurant drinking tea.

Outside, on the *opposite* side of the road, there was a bank. A *security guard* was standing outside the bank.

Len stood up. "I must go," he

站岗

两个失业的人，兰恩和泰德，坐在一家茶馆喝茶。

马路对面有一家银行。一个保安在银行门口站岗。

兰恩站起来说："我必须走了，明天见。"

---

unemployed *adj.* 失业的
security guard 保安

opposite *adj.* 对面的；相反的

CULTURE SERIES

said. "I'll see you tomorrow."

"OK," Ted said. "I'll be here."

Len walked out of the restaurant and crossed the road. Then he walked up to the security guard, said something to him and ran off as fast as he could.

The security guard was very angry and he ran after Len shouting at him.

"Come back here! How dare you *insult* me!" he shouted, but Len kept on running.

The security guard could not catch him and he was soon out of sight.

Still angry, the security guard hurried back to his *position* outside the bank.

泰德说："好的，明天，在这里，不见不散。"

兰恩走出茶馆，穿过马路，走到那个银行保安身边跟他说了点什么，然后撒腿就跑了。

保安非常生气，边追边骂他。

他喊道："回来，你竟敢骂我！"但是，兰恩继续向前跑。

保安追不上他，他很快就不见了。

保安怒气冲冲地回到原来的位置。

---

insult *v.* 侮辱；辱骂   position *n.* 位置；方位

◆ ON GUARD

The next day Len came into the restaurant. Ted was already there. He sat next to him and ordered some tea.

Ted said, "Yesterday, I saw you go up to the security guard, say something to him and run off. He was very angry and ran after you."

"That's right," Len said. "I called him a fat-faced *idiot*. He was really angry."

"Why did you do that?" Ted asked.

"I'm going to rob the bank today," Len said. "I wanted to find out how fast he could run."

第二天,兰恩走进茶馆,泰德已经在那了。他紧挨着兰恩坐下,要了杯茶。

泰德说:"昨天我看见你走到保安身旁,跟他说了点什么,就跑了。他很生气地在后面追你。"

兰恩说:"完全正确,我叫他肥脸白痴,他果真生气了。"

"你为什么那样做啊?"泰德问。

兰恩说:"今天我要去抢银行。我想试试他能跑多快。"

idiot *n.* 白痴;笨蛋

CULTURE SERIES

30

The Cheater

Donald was not very good at math.

He could not understand the teacher's *explanations*.

Even when the teacher *explained* something a second time, Donald still could not understand it.

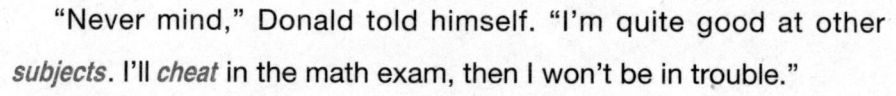

"Never mind," Donald told himself. "I'm quite good at other *subjects*. I'll *cheat* in the math exam, then I won't be in trouble."

作弊者

当诺德数学学得不太好。

他听不懂老师的讲解。

即使老师又给他讲一遍,他还是听不懂。

于是,他自我安慰说:"不要紧,其他科我学得好。数学考试我可以作弊,这样就不会不及格了。"

---

explanation *n.* 解释;说明
subject *n.* 学科;科目

explain *v.* 解释;说明
cheat *v.* 作弊;欺骗

◆ THE CHEATER

"I'll sit next to the boy who's best at math," he thought, "and *copy* down his answers."

The day of the exam came, and Donald sat next to Brian Smith, who was always at the top of the class in math.

Donald carefully copied Brian's answers onto his own exam paper.

At the end of the exam, the teacher collected the papers and graded them.

Then she said, "Well, boys and girls, I've decided to give a *prize* to the student who got the highest grade. It's difficult for me to decide who to give the prize to, however, because two students, Donald and Brian, got the same grade."

他心理盘算着:"考试时,我就坐在数学成绩最好的同学旁边,抄他的答案。"

考试的那天,当诺德坐在布莱恩·史密斯旁边。史密斯在班里数学成绩总是名列前茅。

当诺德认真地把布莱恩的答案抄到他的试卷上。

考试结束后,老师把试卷收上来,给每个同学打分。

试卷批完后,老师向全班同学宣布:"同学们,我决定要奖励数学成绩最高的同学。然而,对我来说,很难下决定奖励谁,因为当诺德和布莱恩两位同学的分数一样高。"

---

copy *v.* 抄袭   prize *n.* 奖;奖品

CULTURE SERIES

"Let them *share* it," one of the other students said.

"I've thought about that," the teacher said, "but I've decided to give the prize to Brian."

Donald was angry when he heard this.

He stood up and said, "That's not *fair*. I got the same grade as Brian."

"That's true," the teacher said. "However, Brian's answer to question 18 was 'I don't know.' Yours was 'Neither do I.'".

一个同学说:"让他们二人共享这个奖励吧。"

老师说:"我也想过这个办法,但还是决定奖励布莱恩。"

听了老师的决定,当诺德非常生气。

他站起来说道:"这不公平,我和布莱恩的分数是一样的。"

老师说:"的确是这样。然而,布莱恩第18题的答案是'我不知道',而你的答案是'我也不知道'。"

---

share *v.* 分享;均分   fair *adj.* 公正的;公平的

The Three Tortoises

Once upon a time, there were three *tortoises* who were friends.

One of them was a large tortoise, one was a *medium*-sized tortoise and the third was a small tortoise.

One day they went into a

三只乌龟

从前，有三只乌龟，他们是好朋友。

他们分别是大乌龟，中等乌龟，和小乌龟。

一天，他们来到一家餐馆并点了些蛋糕。

---

tortoise *n.* 乌龟   medium *adj.* 中等的

CULTURE SERIES

restaurant and ordered some cakes.

While they were waiting for the cake, they remembered that they hadn't brought any money.

"Hey, we forgot to bring money to pay for our cake," the big tortoise said.

"The little tortoise can go home and get it," the medium-sized tortoise said. "He's the youngest, so he should be the one to go."

The little tortoise wasn't very pleased with this, but he knew he shouldn't *argue* with his *elders*, so he said, "All right, I'll go. But you must promise not to eat my cake while I'm away."

The large tortoise and the medium-sized tortoise agreed, and the little tortoise set off for home to get some money.

A few days later, the big tortoise said to the medium-sized

当他们等蛋糕时，才想起来谁也没带钱。

大乌龟说："嗨，我们忘带钱了，怎么结账啊？"

中等乌龟说："让小乌龟回家取钱吧。他最小，所以应该他回去取。"

小乌龟很不高兴，但是他知道争不过另外两只乌龟，就说："那好吧！我回去。但是你们必须答应我，在我离开的时候，不准偷吃我的蛋糕。"

大乌龟和中等乌龟都同意了，小乌龟就回家去取钱了。

几天以后，大乌龟对中等乌龟说："咱们把小乌龟的蛋糕吃了吧！我又饿了！"

---

argue v. 争辩；争论   elder n. （两人中）年龄较大者

tortoise, "Let's eat the little tortoise's cake. I'm hungry again."

"So am I," the medium-sized tortoise said, and reached for the cake.

As he did so, the little tortoise shouted from near the door of the restaurant, "If you *touch* my cake, I won't go get the money!"

中等乌龟说:"我也饿了。"说着说着,就伸手去拿蛋糕。

这时,只听见小乌龟在餐馆门口喊道:"如果你们敢动我的蛋糕,我就不回去取钱了!"

touch *v.* 接触(某事物)

An Old Friend

Carol Evans hated to be wrong. If she made a mistake, she could never *admit* it.

One day, she was walking along the street when she *bumped* into another woman.

She looked at the woman very carefully.

老朋友

开罗·伊万斯讨厌犯错。

如果犯了错,她从来都不会承认。

一天,她走在街上偶然碰见了一位女友。

她仔仔细细地打量了一下这位女友。

---

admit v. (通常不情愿地)承认,供认   bump v. (意外地)撞;撞上(某物)

◆ AN OLD FRIEND

Then she said, "Kate Foster! Well, well, well, I haven't seen you for ten years."

She looked the woman up and down.

"But you've changed, Kate," she went on. "You used to be fat but now you're thin."

She smiled at her, "But you look good and it's nice to see you again."

She took the woman's hand and *shook* it.

"But, oh, you have changed," she said. "I've never known anyone to change so much. You used to have thick hair but now it's very thin. You didn't used to wear glasses but now you're wearing really thick ones."

然后说:"凯特·福斯特!我们有十年没见面了。"

她又上上下下地打量了一番,说:"凯特,你变了。以前你很胖,可现在却瘦了。"

她笑着说:"你看上去也不错,见到你很高兴。"

她们彼此握了握手。

她接着说:"噢,但是你变了,我从来没见过有人变化这么大的。你头发以前又浓又密,可现在变少了。你以前也不戴眼镜,可现在却戴上了厚厚的眼镜。"

---

shake (hands) *v.* 握手

She smiled at the woman again.

"But you're still the same Kate Foster I used to have coffee with every week. We had some good times, didn't we, Kate?"

"Excuse me, ma'am," the woman said, "but my name isn't Kate Foster."

Carol thought for a minute and said, "So you've changed your name as well, have you?"

她又对女友笑了笑。

"但是你还是那个凯特·福斯特,以前我们每周都一起去喝咖啡,还一起度过了许多美好的时光,不是吗,凯特?"

"对不起,女士。我不是凯特·福斯特。"她的女友解释道。

开罗想了一会儿说:"你连名字也改了吗?"

◆ NOT HERE

33

Not Here

Kathy and Polly were friends but they liked playing *tricks* on each other.

One day Kathy met Polly in the street. She said, "Hi, Polly. It's good to see you."

"How can you see me when I'm not here?" Polly asked.

"What do you mean, you're not here?" Kathy asked. "Of course

不在这里

凯瑟和鲍莉是好朋友，但是他们喜欢开玩笑。

一天凯瑟在街上遇见了鲍莉。她说："嗨，鲍莉。很高兴见到你。"

鲍莉问："我不在这里，你怎么看见我的啊？"

凯瑟问："你的意思是你不在这里？但是你不就在这吗？"

---

trick *n.* 把戏；戏法

CULTURE SERIES

you're here."

"No, I'm not," Polly said, "and I'll *bet* you ten dollars that I can *prove* I'm not here."

"All right," said Kathy. "Ten dollars. Now prove you're not here."

"Easy," Polly said. "Am I in Hong Kong?"

"No," said Kathy.

"Am I in Paris?"

"No," said Kathy.

"If I'm not in Hong Kong and I'm not in Paris," Polly said, "then I must be somewhere else. Right?"

"Right," said Kathy. "You must be somewhere else."

"不，我不在这里，"鲍莉说，"我跟你打赌，赌10美元，我可以证明我不在这里。"
"好吧，"凯瑟说，"10美元。现在你就证明你不在这里吧。"
"很简单。"鲍莉说，"我在香港吗？"
"不在，"凯瑟说。
"那我在巴黎吗？"
"不在，"凯瑟说。
"如果我不在香港也不在巴黎，"鲍莉说，"那么我一定在其他地方了，对吧？"
"对呀，"凯瑟说，"你一定在其他地方。"

---

bet v. 打赌　　　　　　　　　　　　　　　　　　prove v. 证明

◆ NOT HERE

"Exactly," said Polly. "And if I'm somewhere else I can't be here, can I? Ten dollars, please."

"That's very *clever*, Polly," Kathy said, "but I can't give you ten dollars."

"Why not?" asked Polly. "We had a bet."

"Certainly we had a bet," Kathy laughed, "but how can I give you ten dollars if you're not here?"

"太对了，"鲍莉说，"如果我在其他地方，那么现在我就不在这里，我说的对吧？10美元，拿来吧！"

"太聪明了，鲍莉。"凯瑟说，"但是我不能给你10美元。"

"为什么不给？"鲍莉说，"我们已经打赌了啊。"

"当然啦，"凯瑟大笑说，"既然你不在这里，我怎么给你钱呀？"

---

clever *adj.* 聪明的

CULTURE SERIES

34

A Bad Doctor

A man walked into a doctor's examining room.

"Put out your *tongue*," the doctor said.

The man put out his tongue and the doctor looked at it quickly.

"OK, you can put your tongue back now," the doctor said. "It's *clear* what's wrong with you. You need more exercise."

不称职的医生

一个病人走进医生的检查室。

"伸出你的舌头。"医生说。

病人伸出了舌头,医生看了一下。

"好的,收回去吧。"医生说,"我知道你得了什么病,你需要多锻炼。"

---

tongue *n.* 舌头　　　　　　　　　clear *adj.* 易懂的;清楚的

◆ A BAD DOCTOR

"But, doctor," the man said, "I don't think..."

"Don't tell me what you think," the doctor said. "I am the doctor, not you. I know what you need. I see hundreds of people like you. None of them get any exercise. They sit in offices all day and in front of the television in the evening. What you need is to walk quickly for *at least* 20 minutes a day."

"Doctor, you don't understand," the patient said. "I ..."

"I don't want to hear any excuses," the doctor said. "You must find time for exercise. If you don't, you will get fat and have health problems when you are older."

"But I walk every day, " the patient said.

"但是，医生，"病人说，"我认为不是……"

"不要告诉我你怎么想的，"医生说，"我是医生。我知道你需要什么。我检查过几百个像你这样的病人。他们中没有一个人爱运动。他们白天坐在办公室，晚上坐在电视机前。你们所需要的只是每天至少快走20分钟。"

"医生，你不明白，"病人说，"我……"

"我不想听任何解释，"医生说，"你必须找时间锻炼一下。如果你不锻炼，老了就会发胖，而且存在许多健康问题。"

"但是我每天都走呀，" 病人说。

---

at least 至少

CULTURE SERIES

"Oh, yes, and I know what kind of walking that is. You walk a few *feet* from your house to the train station, a few more feet from the station to your office, and a few more feet from your office to a restaurant for lunch and back. That's not real walking. I'm talking about a walk in the park for twenty minutes every day."

"Will you listen to me, doctor!" the patient shouted, getting angry with this doctor who thought he knew everything.

"I'm a mailman," the patient went on, "and I walk for seven hours every day!"

For a moment the doctor was *silent*. Then he said quietly, " Put your tongue out again, will you?"

"噢，是的，我知道。你只不过是从家走到火车站，再从火车站走到办公室，又从办公室走到餐馆吃午饭，然后返回。那不是真正的运动，我说的是每天在公园里至少走20分钟。"

"你能先听我说吗？医生！"病人气愤地喊道。

"我是一名邮递员，"病人继续说，"我每天至少要走7个小时！"

医生沉默了一会，然后说："再伸出你的舌头好吗？"

---

foot *n.* 英尺　　　　　　　　　　silent *adj.* 沉默的；不发表意见的

Nothing To Complain About

One day Susan Lee was walking along the street when she saw her friend Lisa Carter.

She had not seen her old friend for some time, so she said, "We've got lots to talk about. Let's have some tea and cake in that *café*."

She pointed to a nearby café.

Lisa agreed, so the two friends went into the café.

没什么可抱怨的

一天，苏珊在街上碰见了她的朋友莉萨。

她俩有很长时间没见面了，因此她说："我们要好好聊聊。这样吧，我们去那家咖啡店，要壶茶和点心怎么样？"

她指着最近的一家咖啡店。

莉萨表示赞同，然后两人就进了那家咖啡店。

---

café *n.* 咖啡馆；小餐馆

CULTURE SERIES

Susan ordered. "We'll have two pieces of cake," she said, "and a *pot* of tea."

The waitress wrote down their order and went away.

She soon returned with the cake and the pot of tea.

Susan saw *immediately* that one piece of cake was a little bigger than the other.

However, she was *well-mannered*, so she picked up the *plate* and offered it to Lisa.

"Have a piece of cake, Lisa," she said.

"Thank you," Lisa said. "But after you."

"No, no," Susan said. "After you, please."

"Very well," Lisa said and she took the bigger of the two pieces of cake.

苏珊点了一壶茶和两块蛋糕。
服务员记下菜单，转身离去。
不久蛋糕和茶水就端上来了。
苏珊立刻注意到有一块蛋糕比另一块大一点。
可她却很有礼貌地把那块大蛋糕让给了莉萨。
"吃蛋糕吧，莉萨。"她说。
"谢谢！"莉萨说，你先来吧。"
"不，不，不！"苏珊说，"还是你先来吧。"
莉萨说："那好吧。"就把大蛋糕拿到自己盘子里了。

---

pot n. 壶
well-mannered adj. 彬彬有礼的

immediately adv. 立刻；马上
plate n. 盘；碟

Susan was angry. "You've taken the bigger piece of cake," she said. "That was very rude."

"Not at all," Lisa *replied*. "Tell me, if you had taken the cake before me, which cake would you have taken?"

"The smaller one, of course," Susan said.

"Exactly. Well, you've got the smaller one, so what are you *complaining* about?"

苏珊很生气。"你把大蛋糕拿走了,"她说,"那是很不礼貌的。"

"不是的,"莉萨回答道,"听我说,如果我让你先拿蛋糕,你拿哪块?"

"当然是小的了。"苏珊说。

"对呀。你既然选择拿小的,那你还抱怨什么呢?"

reply *v.* 回答;答复　　　　　　　　complain *v.* 抱怨;埋怨

CULTURE SERIES

36

A Good-Bye Gift

When Michael Brown died, his three best friends went to his *funeral*.

They stood for a moment, looking down into the *grave* of their friend.

"He was a good friend," the first person said. "He was *generous* and kind. Let's give him some money to use in *heaven*."

The other two friends agreed. They thought this was a good idea.

告别的礼物

当迈克·布朗去世的时候,他三个最好的朋友来参加葬礼。

他们站了一会儿,俯看着朋友的坟墓。

"他是个好朋友,"第一个人说,"活着的时候,非常慷慨和体贴。咱们给他些钱在天堂用吧。"

另两个朋友同意了并认为这是个好主意。

funeral *n.* 葬礼
generous *adj.* 慷慨的;大方的

grave *n.* 坟墓
heaven *n.* 天堂

A GOOD-BYE GIFT

The first friend took his wallet out of his pocket, opened it and took out a hundred-dollar bill. Then he threw it into the grave.

The second friend did not want the other two to think he was *stingy*, so he also took out his wallet.

"You're right," he said. "He always helped his friends. He *deserves* to have everything he needs in his next life."

And with these words, he also threw a hundred-dollar bill into the grave.

The third man looked at the other two, and thought carefully for several minutes. He did not want them to think he was stingy, but he really did hate spending money.

At last, he bent down, took the two hundred-dollar bills out of the grave and put them in his pocket.

第一个朋友从口袋中取出钱夹，拿出100美元，然后扔进了坟墓。

第二个朋友怕别人认为他很小气，也掏出钱夹。

"你说得对，"他说，"他总是帮助朋友。他值得下辈子拥有需要的一切。"说着说着，他也把100美元扔进了坟墓。

第三个人看了看他俩，想了一会儿。他不想让他们知道他很吝啬，但他确实又吝惜花钱。

最后，他弯腰把那200美元从坟墓中拾起来，装进自己的口袋里。

---

stingy　adj. 吝啬的；小气的　　　　　　　　deserve　v. 应受；值得

CULTURE SERIES

Then he took out his checkbook and wrote a *check* for three hundred dollars. He then threw the check into the grave.

"I haven't got any change," he said, "but that check is for three hundred dollars, so I've given the same as you."

然后掏出支票簿，开了一张300美元的支票，扔进坟墓。

"我没有零钱，"他说，"但是我开了张300美元的支票，所以我给的钱和你们一样多。"

---

check *n.* 支票；收据

Good Value

George was very stingy. He hated spending money.

Whenever he had to buy something he always argued about the price and tried to *bargain* even for the cheapest things.

If he wanted to buy a can of Coke, for example, and the shopkeeper asked for $2, George would say,

物有所值

乔治很吝啬，讨厌花钱。

无论买什么，即使是最便宜的东西，他都试图讨价还价。

如果他想买一罐可乐，售货员要两美元，他会说："1.9美元我就买。"

bargain *v.* 讨价还价

CULTURE SERIES

"Make it $1.90 and I'll buy it."

Sometimes the shopkeepers agreed to *reduce* their prices a little. "What's ten *cents*?" they asked themselves. "If it makes this man happy, then it won't hurt me very much."

In this way George saved a few cents here and a few cents there, and by the end of the year he had saved several hundred dollars.

One day he had a very bad toothache and had to go to the *dentist*. The dentist looked at the tooth and said, "This tooth will have to come out. It's too *damaged* to save."

"How much do you charge to take out a tooth?" George asked.

"Forty dollars," the dentist said.

"Forty dollars!" George thought this was much too expensive.

有时候，售货员会降低价格卖给他。"10美分算什么呢？"他们会想，"如果那样能使这人高兴，对我又不会造成太大损失的话。"

乔治用这种方法这里攒几美分，那里攒几美分，一年下来，已经攒了几百美元了。

一天，乔治牙疼得厉害，就去了牙医诊所。牙医检查后说："这颗牙应该拔掉，留着病情会更严重。"

"拔一颗牙要多少钱啊？"乔治问。

"40美元。"牙医说。

"40美元？"乔治认为太贵了。

---

reduce *v.* 减少；缩小；降低
dentist *n.* 牙医

cent *n.* 分；分币
damage *v.* 损伤；损坏

◆ GOOD VALUE

"How long will it take you to pull out the tooth?" he asked.

"About two minutes," the dentist said.

George could not believe what he was hearing. "Forty dollars for two minutes' work!" he shouted. "That's *robbery*."

The dentist smiled. "You're right," she said. "Thank you for telling me. I'll pull your tooth out very slowly. How about if I take half an hour?"

"拔一颗牙多长时间？"他问。

"大约两分钟。"牙医说。

乔治不敢相信他所听到的。"两分钟就40美元！"他喊道，"那不是抢劫嘛！"

牙医笑了笑，"你说得对。"她说，"谢谢你的建议，我可以慢点给你拔，半个小时怎么样啊？"

robbery *n.* 抢劫；盗窃

CULTURE SERIES

38

Not Funny

John Smith and his friend Bill Jones were *shipwrecked* on a *deserted* island in the middle of the Pacific Ocean.

They had plenty of fish and fruit to eat, but nothing to read except a book full of jokes.

Each of the jokes was *numbered*.

At first, to help pass the time, John and Bill read the jokes to one

---

无趣

约翰·史密斯和他的朋友比尔·琼斯遭遇海难，漂流到太平洋中部的一个孤岛上。

在那里，他们有很多鱼和水果可吃，但除了一本笑话书之外，没有什么其他读物了。

每一个笑话都有序号。

起初，为了消磨时光，他们彼此读笑话；后来，他们复述笑话；一年

---

shipwrecked *adj.* 遭遇海难的；船只失事的　　　deserted *adj.* 空无一人的
numbered *v.* 编号；给……标号码

◆ NOT FUNNY

another; then they told them from *memory*. After a year they knew the jokes so well that they just said the number of the joke.

"Twenty," John would say, and Bill would *roar* with laughter.

Then Bill might say, "Seventy-five," and John would laugh.

One day, after they had been on the island for many years, another man was shipwrecked with them.

"How do you pass the time?" he asked them.

"We tell each other jokes." Bill said, and handed him the joke book.

"Tell us a joke," John said. "Just read out the number."

"OK," the man said. He looked through the book until he found a joke he thought was very funny. It was number eighty-three.

后，他们更熟悉这些笑话了，甚至可以直接说出笑话的序号。

约翰要是说："20"，比尔就会狂笑。

比尔说："75"，约翰也会大笑。

他们在岛上居住了很多年后的一天，又有一个人遭遇海难来到这里。

"你们怎么打发时间啊？"他问。

"哦，我们彼此讲笑话。"比尔说，并把笑话书递给了他。

"给我们讲个笑话吧，"约翰说，"你只要说出序号就行。"

"好吧，"这个人说。他看了一遍书，直到找到一个他认为很有意思

---

memory *n.* 记忆　　　　　　　　　　　　roar *v.* 大声表示；大声说

CULTURE SERIES

"I've found a good joke," he said. "Are you ready?"

"Yes," Bill and John said.

"Right," the man said. "Here it is eighty-three."

John and Bill just looked at the man. Their faces did not move. They did not make a sound.

"Why didn't you laugh?" the man asked.

"You didn't tell it very well," Bill said.

的笑话，它的序号是83。

"我找到了一个有意思的笑话了，"他说，"你们准备好了吗？"

"是的。"比尔和约翰说。

"那好，"这个人说，"在这里，83。"

约翰和比尔看着这个人。两人脸上没有表情，也没笑。

"你们为什么不笑呢？"这个人问。

"你还没讲呢？"比尔说。

The Right Tools For the Job

When his young son was ill, Mr Davis took him to a *clinic*. They were the first patients of the day and did not have to wait long.

The *nurse* took the boy into the doctor's room while Mr Davis waited outside.

After a few minutes, the doctor came out of his room and spoke to

看病需要的工具

大卫斯先生的小儿子生病了,他带着儿子来到一家诊所。

他们是那天第一位病人,因此不用久等。

护士带着他儿子进了医生的办公室,而大卫斯先生则在门外等着。

几分钟后,医生从办公室出来对护士说:"有螺丝刀吗?"

---

clinic n. 诊所;门诊部   nurse n. 护士

CULTURE SERIES

the nurse.

"Have we got a *screwdriver*?" he asked her.

The nurse looked in a *drawer* and found a screwdriver.

She gave it to the doctor and he went back into his room.

A few minutes later he came out again, "I need a *saw*," he said to the nurse this time.

Again the nurse looked in the drawer.

She found a saw and gave it to the doctor. He went back into his room.

A few minutes later the doctor came out of his room for the third time.

"I'm going to need a *hammer*," he said.

For the third time the nurse looked in the drawer. She found a hammer and gave it to the doctor.

护士打开抽屉,找到了一把螺丝刀。

她递给医生,医生进去了。

几分钟后他又出来了。"我需要一把锯。"他对护士说。

护士又在抽屉中翻了翻,找到一把锯递给了医生,医生又进去了。

几分钟以后,医生再次从办公室出来。

"我需要锤子。"他说。

护士再次打开抽屉。找到锤子,递给了医生。

---

screwdriver n. 螺丝刀
saw n. 锯子

drawer n. 抽屉
hammer n. 锤子

This time, Mr Davis could not keep quiet.

"Excuse me," he said, "but what is wrong with my son? And what are you doing to him?"

"I haven't *examined* him yet," the doctor said. "I'm still trying to get my bag open."

这次,大卫斯先生忍不住了。

"麻烦问一下,"他说,"我儿子得了什么病?你对他做了些什么?"

"还没检查呢,"医生说,"我得先把箱子打开。"

---

examine *v.* 检查;仔细观察

CULTURE SERIES

40

Paid In Full

One day a bus stopped at a tourist *spot*, and all the *passengers* got out and went into a nearby restaurant.

One of them walked up to the manager and said, "Good morning. I am Mr Tom Wilkins. These people are all patients at the City *Psychiatric*

全单照付

一天，一辆巴士停在一个旅游景点，所有的乘客都下了车，走进附近一家餐馆。

其中一个人跟经理打招呼："早上好！我叫汤姆·威尔克斯。这些人都是市精神病院的病人。他们每年都有一次汽车旅游。他们表现很好，但

---

spot *n.* 地点
psychiatric *adj.* 精神病的；精神病学的

passenger *n.* 乘客

◆ PAID IN FULL

Hospital. They are having their *annual* bus trip. They will all behave very well, but there is one small problem. They will want to pay for their food and drink with *bottle caps*. I'll be *grateful* if you will let them do this, then let me have the bill just before we leave."

The manager wanted to be helpful, so he said, "That will be fine, sir. I hope you will all enjoy yourselves in my restaurant."

The patients all sat down. They ordered their food and drink, and behaved very well. No one knew they were patients at a psychiatric hospital.

At the end of the meal, each of them paid his or her bill with bottle caps.

是有一个小问题，他们得用瓶盖来付款。如果你允许他们这么做，我将不胜感激。在离开前，我会结账的。"

经理也想帮助他们，因此说："那好吧，先生。我希望你们用餐愉快。"

所有的病人都入座了。他们点了食物和饮料，表现得很好。几乎没人看得出他们是精神病人。

吃完饭后，他们都起身用瓶盖付账。

---

annual *adj.* 每年的；一年一次的 bottle cap 瓶盖
grateful *adj.* 感激的；感谢的

CULTURE SERIES

Then they left the restaurant and got back on the bus.

Tom Wilkins went up to the manager. "You've been most kind," he said, "and understanding. I'll pay the bill now."

The manager *added* up everything the patients had *ordered*, and gave the total to Tom. It came to quite a lot of money.

"That's a fair price," Tom said. "I'm happy to pay that. Have you got change for six bottles?"

然后他们离开餐馆回到巴士上。

汤姆·威尔克斯来到经理面前。"你心地很善良,"他说,"也很善解人意。结账吧。"

经理把账单递给了汤姆。那是很大一笔钱。

"价钱还比较合理,"汤姆说。"我愿意支付。我付给你6个瓶子,你能找零吗?"

---

add v. 加;增加   order v. (饭店等)叫(饭菜等)

41

The Wrong Question

One day when Jack was walking in the park, he saw a woman he knew sitting on a *bench* with a dog beside her. The dog was looking up at the woman.

Jack walked up to the woman and said, "Hello, Sue, how are you? May I sit and talk with you for a while?"

"Of course, please sit down," Sue said.

错误的问题

一天,杰克在公园散步,碰见一位认识的妇女坐在长凳上,旁边还有一条狗。这条狗一直盯着这个妇女。

杰克走到妇女面前说:"嗨,苏!最近怎么样?可以坐下和你聊一会儿吗?"

"当然,请坐。"苏说。

---

bench *n.* 长凳

CULTURE SERIES

Jack sat down next to Sue on the bench, and they talked quietly together.

The dog continued to look up at Sue, as if waiting to be *fed*.

"That's a nice dog," Jack said, pointing at the animal.

"Yes, he's handsome. He's a bit of a *mixture*, but that's not a bad thing. He's strong and healthy."

"And hungry," Jack said. "He hasn't taken his eyes off you. He thinks you've got some food for him."

"That's true," Sue said. "But I haven't."

The two friends laughed and then Jack said, "Does your dog *bite*?"

杰克在苏旁边坐了下来。他们轻声地交谈着。

那条狗继续望着苏,好像在等着她喂食。

"真是条讨人喜欢的狗。"杰克指着那条狗说。

"是的,它很好看。有一点像混种狗,但也不是件坏事。它很强壮也很健康。"

"而且很饿,"杰克说,"它的眼睛从未离开过你,好像等你喂食呢。"

"是的,"苏说,"但我没有食物。"

两个人大笑,然后杰克说:"你的狗会咬人吗?"

---

feed *v.* 喂养;饲养   mixture *n.* 混合物;混合状态
bite *v.* 咬

◆ THE WRONG QUESTION

"No," Sue said. "He's never bitten anyone. He's always *gentle* and good-tempered."

Hearing this, Jack decided to *pet* the dog. He put out his hand and touched the animal's head. Immediately it jumped up and bit him.

"Hey!" Jack shouted. "You said your dog didn't bite."

Sue replied, "That's not my dog. My dog's at home."

"不，"苏说，"它从来不咬人，总是很温顺，脾气也很好。"

听到这，杰克想拍一下这条狗。他伸出手抚摸着这条狗的脑袋。狗立刻跳起来咬他。

"嘿！"杰克喊，"你不是说你家狗不咬人吗？"

苏回答道，"那不是我的狗，我的狗在家呢。"

---

gentle *adj.* 温和的；温顺的   pet *v.* 抚摸；爱抚

CULTURE SERIES

42

Bananas Are Bad for You

Pearl and June were good friends and spent most of their time together.

They were both very old and they worried about their health. Most of the time they talked about nothing else.

They worried about their food.

坏香蕉

珀尔和朱恩是多年好友,她们大部分时间都待在一起。

她们都上年纪了,很担心自己健康,大部分时间都在讨论健康问题。

她们担心食物是否干净?是否对胃不好?

◆ BANANAS ARE BAD FOR YOU

Was it clean? Would it give them stomach pains?

They worried about the weather. Was it too cold and wet? Would it give them pains in their bones?

They worried about *pollution* in the air. Would it give them pains in their *chests* and throats?

They worried about being hurt in a car *accident*, killed in an airplane *crash*, getting sick, and so on.

All they could think about was being ill or hurt.

One day they went on a train journey together.

"We'll need some food," Pearl said.

"We'll buy some bananas," June said. "They are good to eat and always clean."

她们担心天气是否太冷太潮？会不会患风湿？

她们担心空气污染是否会伤害肺和嗓子？

她们担心交通事故、坠机、生病等等。

她们认为所有的东西都会导致疾病或者受到伤害。

一天，她们一起坐火车旅行。

"我们需要带些食物。"珀尔说。

"我们买一些香蕉吧，"朱恩说，"既好吃又干净。"

---

pollution *n.* 污染　　　　　　　　　　chest *n.* 胸部
accident *n.* 意外事故；事件　　　　　crash *n.* （飞机）失事

CULTURE SERIES

And so they bought two bananas to eat on the train.

It was not long before they were hungry.

Pearl took out the bananas and gave one to June. Then she *peeled* the skin of her banana and took a large bite of it.

At that moment the train went into a *tunnel*. Everything went black.

"Don't eat your banana," Pearl shouted at June. "Mine has made me go *blind*!"

所以她们买了两个香蕉准备在火车上吃。

不久她们就饿了。

珀尔拿出香蕉，分给朱恩一个。然后她剥开香蕉，吃了一大口。

这时候火车正好进入了隧道，一切都黑了。

"你不要吃香蕉了，"珀尔对朱恩喊到。"香蕉已经让我失明了。"

peel v. 削去（水果、蔬菜的）皮　　　　tunnel n. 地道；隧道
blind adj. 盲的

Big John

Once in the old days of the American West, a small man suddenly ran into a hotel. It was full of men drinking and talking.

The small man was very frightened.

"Big John's coming," he shouted. "Run for your lives!"

Immediately every man put down his drink and ran out of the hotel. The *bartender* hid under the *bar*.

大约翰

很早以前,在美国西部的一家旅馆,坐满了喝酒聊天的人。这时,一个小矮个突然闯了进来。

小矮个一副被吓坏了的样子。

"大约翰来了,"他喊道。"快逃命。"

大家都立刻放下酒杯,跑出旅馆。酒保则藏在吧台下面。

---

bartender *n.* 酒保;酒吧侍者　　　　bar *n.* 酒吧

CULTURE SERIES

Everyone had heard of Big John and was afraid of him.

It was not long before the door of the hotel opened and a huge man walked in.

He was taller and fatter than two men together and he had two guns on his *hips*.

He had hands the size of shovels, a thick, black beard and *evil*-looking eyes.

He stood by the door and looked around the room, then slowly he walked towards the bar.

"Thump! Thump!" went the sound of his feet on the floor.

The bartender heard him coming and began to *shake*.

The man reached the bar. He *leaned* over it and looked down at the shaking bartender.

大家都听说过大约翰，都很怕他。
不久，旅馆的门被踢开了，进来一个彪形大汉。
他有两个人个头那么高，还很胖，胯间别着两把枪。
他有一双铲子大小的手，又黑又密的胡子和一双邪恶的眼睛。
他站在门口，环视四周，慢慢来到吧台前。
双脚落地的声音如重锤凿地"嘭、嘭、嘭"。
酒保听着他走近的声音，便开始发抖。
他走过来，倚着吧台，看见躲在吧台下浑身发抖的酒保。

---

hip *n.* 臀部；骨宽部
shake *v.* 发抖；打战

evil *adj.* 邪恶的；有害的
lean *v.* 倚靠

◆ BIG JOHN

He took a deep *breath*. The bartender was sure his last hour had come.

Then the man spoke in a deep, loud voice that made the whole room *shake*.

"You'd better get out of here," he said. "Big John's coming."

酒保深呼一口气，确信自己的末日到了。

这个人嗓音特别洪亮，以至于整个房间都在摇晃。

"你最好给我滚开，"他说，"大约翰就要来了。"

---

breath n. （呼吸的）空气 　　　　　　shake v. （使）摇动；震动

CULTURE SERIES

44

The Wrong Medicine

A farmer had a very *valuable* cow. He took very good care of this cow and one day when it was ill, he was very worried. He telephoned the *vet*.

"What's the problem?" the vet asked him when he arrived.

"My cow's very sick," the farmer said. "I don't know what's the matter with her. She's lying down and

吃错药

农夫有一头很珍贵的母牛。他精心照顾着这头母牛，一天，这头母牛生病了，他非常着急，就给兽医打电话。

当兽医赶到时，问他："出什么事了？"

"牛病了，"农夫说，"我不知道她怎么啦。她总躺着，不起来，也不吃东西，还发出奇怪的声音。"

---

valuable *adj.* 很值钱的；贵重的   vet *n.* 兽医

◆ THE WRONG MEDICINE

won't stand up. She won't eat, and she's making a strange noise."

The vet looked at the cow.

"She's certainly sick," he said, "and she needs to take some very strong medicine."

He took a bottle out of his case, and put two *pills* into his hand.

"Give her these," he said. "They should make her better."

"How should I give them to her?" the farmer asked.

The vet gave him a long *tube*.

"Put this tube in her mouth," he said, "then put the pills in the tube and *blow*. That'll make her *swallow* them."

The vet went away.

兽医给母牛做了检查。
"她一定是病了，"他说，"需要吃些强效药。"
他从医药箱里拿出一瓶药，倒出两粒给农夫。
"给她吃这些药，"他说，"吃完就好了。"
"我怎么喂她吃呢？"农夫问。
兽医拿出一个长试管。
"把这个试管放进她嘴里，"他说，"然后把药放进试管里，一吹就可以让牛把药咽进去了。"
兽医离开了。

---

pill *n.* 药丸；药片
blow *v.* （从嘴里）吹出
tube *n.* 管子；筒
swallow *v.* 吞下；咽下

CULTURE SERIES

The next day he came to the farm again. The farmer was sitting outside his house looking very *miserable*.

"How's your cow?" the vet asked.

"No change," the farmer said, "and I'm feeling very strange myself."

"Oh?" the vet said. "Why?"

"I did what you said," the farmer *explained*. "I put the tube in the cow's mouth and then put two pills down it."

"And?" the vet asked.

"The cow blew first," the farmer said.

第二天兽医又来到农场。农夫坐在门外，看上去很难受。

"牛怎么样了？"兽医问。

"没变化，"农夫说。"倒是我现在觉得怪怪的。"

"哦？"兽医不解地问。"为什么？"

"我按你说的做了，"农夫解释说。"我把试管放进牛的嘴里，然后把两粒药也放进去啦。"

"然后呢？"兽医问。

"牛先吹了。"农夫说。

---

miserable *adj.* 很不幸的；痛苦的   explain *v.* 解释；说明

Something in the Ear

A woman woke up one morning with a bad *earache*. The pain was so bad that she went to see a doctor.

She had to wait a long time in the doctor's waiting room because he was very busy.

While she was waiting, the pain got worse.

Also a piece of *string* began to *grow* out of her ear.

耳朵里的东西

一个妇女早晨起床,觉得耳朵疼得厉害。最后难以忍受,就去看医生了。

可医生却很忙,让她等了很久。

等候时,她的疼痛加剧了。

然后一根绳从她的耳朵里长了出来。

---

earache *n.* 耳痛
grow *v.* 生长

string *n.* 绳,线

CULTURE SERIES

When the doctor saw her, he was very surprised.

"There seems to be a piece of string coming out of your ear," he said.

Carefully he began to pull the string. Inch by inch, he pulled the piece of string out of her ear. Then it would not come any further.

"There seems to be something at the end of the string," the doctor said. "I'll have to pull harder."

He began to pull harder, but the pain was so great the woman asked him to stop.

"I must take out whatever is in your ear," the doctor told her. "I'll give you something to help you sleep while I take it out."

The doctor gave the woman sleeping gas, and soon she was in a

---

当医生看见她时，十分惊讶。

"好像有一根绳从你耳朵里长出来了。"医生说。

他开始仔细地拽绳。一寸一寸地，把绳从耳朵里拽出来。后来就拽不动了。

"似乎绳的另一端有什么东西，"医生说。"我必须更用力拽出来。"

他开始用力拽，但是太疼了，妇女就让医生停了下来。

"我必须拽出你耳朵里的东西，"医生告诉她。"我会给你催眠，然后再把它取出来。"

医生向妇女喷洒了催眠气，她很快就睡熟了。

---

inch *n.* 英寸（一英尺的十二分之一，约0.025米）

◆ SOMETHING IN THE EAR

deep sleep.

He called his nurse to help him, and together they pulled on the piece of string.

Suddenly there was a sound, and out of the woman's ear came a large *bunch* of roses.

The doctor was very surprised. He had never seen anything like this before.

When the woman woke up, he said, "I pulled a large bunch of roses out of your ear. Do you know where they came from?"

"Wasn't there a card with them?" the woman asked him.

他把护士找来帮忙，和他一起拽绳的另一端。

突然从这个女人的耳朵里拽出一束玫瑰花。

医生非常惊讶。以前可从来没有发生过这样的事情。

妇女醒来后，医生对她说："我从你耳朵里拽出一大把玫瑰，你知道花从哪里来的吗？"

"花里没有卡片吗？"妇女问道。

---

bunch *n.* 束；卷；团

CULTURE SERIES

46

Counting Chickens

It was Mary's birthday. She received a letter from her uncle, who was a farmer.

"Dear Mary," the letter said. "Happy Birthday. I am sending you some chickens. They will arrive tomorrow. I hope you like them. Best wishes, Uncle Toby."

Mary was very pleased. She liked eating eggs. and she liked

数小鸡

今天是玛丽的生日。她收到了来自农场叔叔的一封信。

"亲爱的玛丽,"叔叔在信中写道,"生日快乐！我送你一些小鸡作为礼物。明天就会送到你手里,希望你喜欢。美好的祝愿！叔叔托比。"

玛丽非常高兴,因为她很喜欢吃鸡蛋和鸡肉。她想:"我可以养着这些小鸡,让它们下蛋,然后吃肉。"

eating chicken. "I can keep the chickens for their eggs or eat them," she thought.

When the chickens arrived the next day, they were in a box.

Mary was very *excited*. She took the box off the back of the truck and began to carry it back to her house.

However, the box of chickens was heavy and she *dropped* it. The box fell to the ground and broke. The chickens all ran out.

They ran everywhere—into neighbors' gardens, into the road, into shops, even into the next street. Mary spent hours trying to find them and take them back to her garden.

A few days later, her uncle came to visit her.

"Did the chickens arrive safely?" he asked Mary.

第二天，小鸡送到玛丽手里，它们都装在盒子里。

玛丽非常激动，她从卡车上取下盒子，向屋里走去。

但盒子太重了，一不小心就从玛丽的手里掉了下去。

盒子掉在地上摔破了，小鸡一下子跑开了。

小鸡跑的到处都是，有的跑进了邻居的花园，有的跑上了马路，跑进了商店，有的甚至跑向了邻街。

玛丽花了好几小时才把这些小鸡找回来，把它们带回了花园。

几天后，叔叔来看她。

"小鸡都安全到达了吧？"叔叔问玛丽。

---

excited *adj.* 兴奋的　　　　　　　　　　　　drop *v.* 落下；扔下

CULTURE SERIES

"Yes, Uncle Toby," Mary said. "But I had a lot of trouble with them. I dropped the box. It broke open and the chickens ran everywhere. I *spent* the whole morning looking for them."

"Did you find them all?" her uncle asked.

"I hope so," Mary *replied*. "I caught eleven of them."

"That's very interesting," her uncle said with a smile, "because I only sent you six."

"是的，托比叔叔。"玛丽说，"可这些小鸡给我带来了不少麻烦。我不小心把盒子摔破了，小鸡跑得到处都是。我花了整个早晨才把它们找回来。"

"都找到了吗？"叔叔问道。

"希望如此。"玛丽回答道，"我一共找回11只。"

"那可真有趣！"叔叔笑着说，"我只送给你6只啊。"

---

spend　*v.*　花（时间）；花费

reply　*v.*　回答

A Housing Problem

Sue and Alan had been *dating* for many years. Every *weekend* they went to a movie together on Saturday night. On Sundays they went to the beach in the summer and to the country in the winter.

Sue knew that Alan wanted to marry her, and she wanted to marry Alan. She waited *patiently* for him to ask her to marry him.

住房困难

苏和艾伦约会有好几年了。每个周末,他们都一起去看电影,夏季的周日一起去海滩,冬季的周日则一起去乡下。

苏知道艾伦想娶她,她也想嫁给艾伦。她一直耐心地等着艾伦的求婚。

date *v.* 约会
patiently *adv.* 耐心地

weekend *n.* 周末

CULTURE SERIES

However, although he often told her he loved her, he never said anything about marriage.

This made Sue unhappy. She was nearly thirty. She believed that if Alan did not marry her soon, she might never marry. She did not want to be a *spinster*. She wanted to have a husband and a family of her own.

One evening, as they were walking home after a *movie*, she said, "Alan, don't you think it is time you asked me something?"

Alan thought for a moment. He knew what she was thinking about. At last he said, "I'm sorry, Sue, but I don't think I have anything to ask you at this time."

"Then I will have to ask you, Alan," Sue said. "I cannot wait any longer. I'm getting old."

She stopped walking and looked at him.

可尽管艾伦一直告诉苏他很爱她，却从没提过结婚的事。

这让苏非常不高兴，她快30岁了，她想，如果不尽快结婚，可能就嫁不出去了。她可不想当老处女，她想拥有丈夫和家。

一天晚上，当他们看完电影往家走时，苏问："艾伦，你不认为现在该向我问点什么事吗？"

艾伦想了一会儿，他知道苏正在想什么，最后他说："我很抱歉，苏，但我想此刻没有什么事要问你。"

"那么，艾伦，我不得不问你了，"苏说道，"我不能再等了，我正在一点点地变老。"

她停下来，盯着艾伦。

---

spinster *n.* 老处女；老姑娘　　　　　　movie *n.* 电影；影片

◆ A HOUSING PROBLEM

"Alan," she said, "we've known each other for ten years. I love you and you love me. Will you marry me?"

Alan took hold of Sue's hand. "Sue," he said, "I want to marry you, but we cannot get married yet. We have nowhere to live. I do not have much money and neither do you. We cannot buy a place of our *own*."

"That isn't important," Sue said. "We can live with your parents."

Alan shook his head. "I'm sorry but that isn't possible."

"Why not?" Sue asked.

"Because my parents are still living with their parents," he *explained*.

"艾伦,"她说,"我们已经认识10年了,我爱你,你也爱我,你愿意娶我吗?"

艾伦捧起苏的手说:"苏,我很想娶你,但现在还不行,我们没有房子,没有很多钱,你也是这样,我们根本没有能力买一栋属于自己的房子。"

"那不重要,"苏说道,"我们可以与你的父母住一起啊。"

艾伦摇摇头说:"很抱歉,那是不可能的事。"

"为什么?"苏问。

"因为我的父母还和他们的父母住一起呢。"艾伦解释说。

---

own *adj.* 自己的　　　　　　　　　　　explain *v.* 解释;说明

48

Dirty Hands

"Have you washed your hands and face?" Billy's mother asked him.

"Yes," he said.

"Show me."

He showed his mother his hands.

"They are *filthy*," she said. "And your face is *covered* in dirt."

脏手

"你洗手洗脸了吗?"妈妈问比尔。

"洗了。"比尔回答。

"给我看看。"

他把手伸出来。

"手脏兮兮的,脸上也尽是灰。"妈妈说。

---

filthy *adj.* 脏的;污秽的

cover *v.* 覆盖某物

◆ DIRTY HANDS

She pulled him into the bathroom. "Now wash your face and hands," she said.

He did as she told him, but he hated doing it.

"Are you *afraid* of soap and water?" his mother asked him.

"No, I'm not afraid of them," he said. "I just don't like them. I hate washing."

When he left the house he was clean. By the time he got to school he was dirty again.

"Look at you!" his teacher *shouted*. "Your face is filthy. If your hands are dirty too, you'll be in *trouble*. Hold out your hands."

Billy knew his hands were dirty. He quickly spit on one and *rubbed* it on his pants. Then he showed it to the teacher.

她把比尔拉进卫生间对他说:"洗洗手和脸。"
比尔照妈妈说的做了,但他讨厌这样做。
"难道你害怕香皂和水吗?"妈妈问。
"不,我不害怕它们,"比尔说,"我讨厌洗漱。"
当比尔离开家时,他是干干净净的。可到学校,又变得脏兮兮的了。
"看看你!"老师冲他喊道,"脸是脏的,如果手也是脏的,你就会有麻烦了,把手伸出来。"
比尔知道他的手很脏,他很快在一只手上吐了点口水并在短裤上擦了擦,然后把手伸出来。

---

afraid *adj.* 恐惧的;害怕的
trouble *n.* 麻烦

shout *v.* 喊;叫
rub *v.* 擦;揩拭

CULTURE SERIES

"That is not a clean hand, Billy," she said. "It's the dirtiest hand in the class. I'm going to *punish* you."

Billy looked around the class. "It's not the dirtiest hand in the class," he said.

"All right, Billy," the teacher said. "If you can show me a dirtier hand, I won't punish you."

With a smile, Billy quickly showed her his other hand.

"比尔,那可不是一只干净的手,"老师说道,"那是同学中最脏的一只手,我得惩罚你。"

比尔向班级四周看了看说:"这不是最脏的手。"

"好的,比尔,"老师说道,"如果你能找出一只更脏的手,我就不罚你了。"

比尔笑了笑,很快地把另一只手伸向了老师。

---

punish *v.* 处罚;惩罚

The Guitar Player

One day Tony Campbell was crossing the road when he was hit by a car. He fell and *broke* his arm.

An *ambulance* soon arrived and took Tony to a hospital. There a doctor *operated* on his arm. Then he put the arm in a *cast*. Tony could not move it at all.

吉他手

一天，托尼·坎贝尔过马路时被车撞了，摔伤了胳膊。

一辆救护车很快赶到，把他送到了医院。在医院，医生给他做完手术后，把他的手放进石膏铸模里，胳膊一点也动弹不了。

---

break *v.* 折断……的骨头
operate *v.* 开刀；动手术
ambulance *n.* 救护车
cast *n.* 石膏；硬质敷料

CULTURE SERIES

"You must keep your arm in a cast for six weeks," the doctor said. "That will give the broken bone a *chance* to *heal*."

At the end of six weeks, Tony went back to the hospital. The doctor used a large saw to cut the cast. Then he took Tony's arm out of the cast.

"Can you move your arm, Tony?" he asked.

Tony tried to move his arm. At first it was difficult, but soon he could move it easily.

"Yes, it's fine," he said. "Thank you very much."

"你的胳膊必须固定在石膏里6周时间，"医生说，"那样骨头才能愈合。"

6周后，托尼来到医院。医生用一把大锯把石膏锯开，然后把他的胳膊从石膏中取出来。

医生问："托尼，胳膊能动吗？"

托尼试着动了动胳膊。一开始有点困难，但很快就能活动自如了。

"很好，"他说，"非常感谢您。"

chance n. 机会   heal v. 治愈；医治

◆ THE GUITAR PLAYER

"In a few days it will be as good as new," the doctor said. "Just *exercise* it a little."

"Will I be able to play the *guitar*?" Tony asked.

The doctor smiled. "Of course you will," he said. "You'll have no problems."

"That is good news," Tony said, "because I couldn't play it at all before."

"再过几天,你的胳膊就跟原来一样了,多运动运动。"医生说。

"我能弹吉他吗?"托尼问道。

医生笑笑说:"当然能啦,一点问题也没有。"

"那可是个好消息,"托尼说,"因为我以前根本不会弹吉他的。"

---

exercise *v.* 锻炼　　　　　　　　　　　　　　guitar *n.* 吉他

CULTURE SERIES

50

School Days

Alice Mancosh was very worried about her son John. He was often *unhappy*.

One morning she walked into his room, *turned on* the light, and said, "It's time to get up, John. You can't stay in bed all day."

John *turned over* in bed. He did not want to get up. He *turned off*

上课日

艾丽斯·曼考什非常替儿子约翰担心,因为他经常不快乐。

一天早上,她走进他房间,把灯打开,说:"约翰,该起床了,你总不能一整天都躺在床上啊。"

约翰翻了翻身。他不想起床,于是把灯关掉了。

unhappy *adj.* 不快乐的;不高兴
turn over 翻;翻过

turn on 打开;开启(设备)
turn off 关掉;关闭(设备)

◆ SCHOOL DAYS

the light.

"Don't go back to sleep," Alice said. "Get up now or you'll be late again for school." She turned the light on again.

Fifteen minutes later John came into the kitchen and sat down at the table.

"Eat your breakfast quickly," Alice said. "It's almost eight thirty."

"There's no *hurry*," John told his mother. "I'm not going to school today."

"Why not?" his mother asked. "Is it a *holiday*?"

John shook his head. "No, it's not a holiday."

Alice sat down next to her son and took his hand.

"John," she said, "tell me what's wrong. Why do you hate school

---

"不要再睡了，"艾丽斯说："快起床，不然又迟到了。"她又打开了灯。

15分钟后，约翰来到厨房，坐在桌子旁。

"快点吃早饭，"艾丽斯说，"都快八点半了。"

"不用急，"约翰对他妈妈说，"我今天不打算去学校。"

"为什么？"他妈妈问，"今天放假吗？"

约翰摇摇头说；"不，不是。"

艾丽斯坐到儿子旁边，握住他的手说："约翰，告诉我发生了什么事，你为什么那么讨厌学校？"

---

hurry　n. 匆忙；急急忙忙　　　　　　　　holiday　n. 假期；假日

CULTURE SERIES

so much?"

For several moments John was *silent*. Then he said, "The teachers *bully* me and the students don't like me."

"John," his mother said, "I'm sorry about that, but you cannot stay at home."

"Why not?" he asked.

"There are two very good *reasons* you must go to school," his mother said. "First, you are thirty-five years old. Second, you are the school *principal*."

约翰沉默了一会儿，然后说：“老师欺负我，学生们也不喜欢我。”
"约翰，"妈妈说，"对此我很难过，但你不能待在家里。"
"为什么不能？"他问。
"有两个非常好的理由。"妈妈说，"首先，你已经35岁了；第二，你是校长。"

---

silent *adj.* 沉默的；安静的
reason *n.* 原因；理由

bully *v.* 欺负；威吓
principal *n.* 校长

◆ IMPORTANCE

51

Importance

Several years ago, a television *reporter* was talking to three of the most important people in the United States.

One was a rich *banker*, another owned one of the largest companies in the world, and the third owned many buildings in the center of New York.

人的重要性

几年前，一名电视记者采访三个比较重要的美国人。

一位是富有的银行家，另一位是世界上最大的公司之一的总裁，第三位则在纽约市中心拥有许多大楼。

---

reporter *n.* 记者   banker *n.* 银行家

CULTURE SERIES

The reporter was talking to them about being important.

"How do we know if someone is really important?" the reporter asked the banker.

The banker thought for a few moments and then said, "I think anyone who is invited to the *White House* to meet the *President* of the United States is really important."

The reporter turned to the owner of the very large company. "Do you *agree* with that?" she asked.

The owner of the very large company shook her head. "No," she said, "I don't, I think the President invites a lot of people to the White House. You'd only be important if while you were visiting the President, there was a telephone call from the President of *Russia*,

---

记者与他们谈论关于重要性的问题。

"我们怎么才能知道一个人真正的重要性呢？"记者问银行家。

银行家想了一会说："我认为任何一个被邀请到白宫与美国总统会面的人是真正重要的人。"

记者转向大公司总裁问："您同意他的观点吗？"

总裁摇摇头说："不，我不这样认为。我认为总统会邀请很多人去白宫。当你正拜访总统时，俄罗斯总统打来电话，而美国总统却说他现在太忙而不能接电话，这才能看出你的唯一重要性。"

White House n. 白宫(美国总统的办公楼)
agree v. 同意；赞成

president n. 总统
Russia n. 俄罗斯

◆ IMPORTANCE

and the President of the United States said he was too busy to answer it."

The reporter turned to the person who owned many buildings. "Do you agree with that?"

"No, I don't," he said. "I don't think that makes the visitor important. That makes the President important."

"Then what would make the visitor important?" the reporter asked.

"Oh, I think if the visitor to the White House was talking to the President and the phone rang, and the President picked it up, listened and then said, 'It's for you.' That's really important."

记者又转向那位拥有许多大楼的人问:"您同意她的观点吗?"

"不,我不那样认为,"他说,"那并不见得来访者有多么重要,那会使总统显得很重要。"

"那么,怎样才能使来访者显得重要呢?"记者问。

"嗯,我认为如果来白宫拜访的人正在与总统说话时,电话响了,总统接起电话,然后说:'您的电话',这样的人才是真正重要的人。"

CULTURE SERIES

52

Nothing Unusual

A horse walked into an expensive restaurant. The head waiter came up to him.

"Good evening," he said.

"I'd like a table for one please," the horse said.

"Have you made a *reservation*?" the waiter asked.

"Yes," the horse said, "I phoned. My name is Running Boy."

"Of course," the waiter said. "This way please, Running Boy."

没什么奇怪的

一匹马走进一家非常昂贵的餐馆，餐馆领班走过来说："早上好。"

"请给我一张单人桌。"这匹马说。

"您提前预订了吗？"领班问。

"是的，"这匹马说，"我打过电话，我是飞毛腿。"

"哦，这边请，飞毛腿。"领班说。

---

reservation *n.* 预定；预约

◆ NOTHING UNUSUAL

He led the horse to a good table by the window. The horse sat down and the waiter *handed* him the *menu*.

"I'd like a *steak* please," the horse said. "*Well-done* with a potato and salad."

"Certainly," the waiter said, and went away.

A little later he returned with the meal and put it on the table in front of the horse.

"Enjoy your meal," he said to the horse and walked away.

The horse ate the meal, and enjoyed it very much. Then he asked the waiter for the bill.

When the waiter gave it to him, the horse said, "You must think it's very unusual. a horse coming into your restaurant and ordering a steak well-done."

"Not at all," the waiter said. "I like it cooked that way myself."

他领着这匹马来到靠窗一个很好的桌位，马坐下后，服务员便递上了一份菜单。

"请给我一份牛排，"马说，"全熟的，外加土豆和沙拉。"

"好的。"领班说完就离开了。

不一会，服务员端来食物放在桌子上。

"祝您用餐愉快。"说完后就离开了。

马吃得很愉快，最后让服务员结账。

服务员把账单递上时，马说："你一定认为很奇怪吧———匹马来这里点了一份全熟的牛排。"

"一点也不啊，"服务员说，"我也喜欢吃全熟的牛排。"

---

hand *v.* 递给　　　　　　　　　　menu *n.* 菜单
steak *n.* 牛排　　　　　　　　　well-done *adj.* 全熟的

Free Tickets

John and Sylvia were quite rich. They had a large beautiful house full of expensive *paintings*.

They had many friends and were not surprised when they received two free tickets for the *theater*. They were surprised,

免费票

约翰和西尔维亚非常有钱。他们拥有一座又大又漂亮的房子，房子里挂满了昂贵的画。

他们有很多朋友，当他们收到两张剧院的免费票时，一点也没惊讶。但是他们惊讶的是不知道是谁送的，因为信封中只有票，没有信。

---

painting n. 画

theater n. 剧院；剧场

◆ FREE TICKETS

however, when they could not find out who had sent them the tickets. There was no letter in the *envelope* with the tickets.

"They've forgotten to put a letter in," John said. "How strange. We don't know who to thank."

They phoned many of their friends and asked, "Did you send us theater tickets?"

"No," their friends said. "We didn't send them."

"It's strange," Sylvia told her husband, "but we shouldn't *waste* the tickets. Everyone says that the play is very good."

And so they went to the theater. They did not really enjoy the play, however, because they were worrying all the time.

"他们一定是忘了把信放进去，"约翰说，"多奇怪呀，我们都不知道该感谢谁。"

他们给许多朋友打电话问："你给我们寄戏票了吗？"

"没有，"朋友回答说，"没寄过。"

"真是奇怪，"西尔维亚对丈夫说："但是我们不能把票浪费了，大家都说这部戏剧不错。"

于是他俩来到了剧院。但他们没能真正享受这部戏剧，因为他们一直在思考这件事。

---

envelope *n.* 信封   waste *v.* 浪费

CULTURE SERIES

The play started at eight o'clock and finished at half past ten. When they got home it was after eleven.

There was a *note* on their front door.

It said, "We hope you enjoyed the play."

Inside the house there was not a *single* painting. They had all been *stolen*.

这部剧8点开始，10点半结束，当他们到家时，已经是11点多了。

他们发现家门上贴着一张纸条。

上面写着："希望你们喜欢这部戏。"

而屋内所有的画都不见了，都被偷光了。

---

note *n.* 短笺；便条   single *adj.* 单一的；唯一的

steal *v.* 偷

54

A Fishy Story

Barry Parker was a very *successful businessman*. He lived in a large house and drove a big car. He wore expensive clothes and ate his meals in famous restaurants. His name was often in the newspapers.

One day a newspaper reporter asked him, "What is the *secret* of your *success*?"

关于鱼的故事

巴里·帕克是位非常成功的商人，住着很大的房子，开着名贵的车，穿着名贵的衣服，在有名的餐馆中就餐，他的名字几乎每天都出现在报纸上。

一天，一个报社记者问他："您成功的秘密是什么呢？"

---

successful *adj.* 成功的；有成果的
secret *n.* 秘密

businessman *n.* 商人
success *n.* 成功；胜利

CULTURE SERIES

Barry thought for a few moments and said, "I eat a *special* kind of fish."

"You eat a special kind of fish!" the reporter said. "What does that do?"

"It makes my *brain* work better," Barry said.

"What kind of fish is it?" the reporter asked.

"Give me fifty dollars and come back tomorrow. I'll have some for you."

The reporter gave Barry fifty dollars and returned the next day.

"Have you got my special fish?" she asked.

"Yes. Come into the house. It's in the refrigerator."

巴里想了一会说:"我吃了一种特殊的鱼。"

"你吃了一种特殊的鱼!"记者说,"那鱼有什么用处呢?"

"它使我的大脑更灵活,"巴里说。

"什么鱼?"记者问。

"给我50美元,明天再来找我,我会给你准备一些的。"

记者给了巴里50美元后,第二天又来找他。

"您给我带那种特殊的鱼了吗?"她问。

"是的,进屋来拿吧,鱼在冰箱里。"

---

special *adj.* 特别的   brain *n.* 大脑

◆ A FISHY STORY

Barry took the reporter into his kitchen. He opened the refrigerator and took out a very small fish. "Here you are. Have this for dinner."

The next day the reporter called on Barry again.

"Did you eat the fish?" Barry asked her.

"Yes, I fried it."

"Good. Do you *feel* different today?"

"No, I don't. And I think that fifty dollars was a lot to pay for such a small fish."

"Well done!" Barry said. "You see, the fish is working. You're using your brain now."

巴里把记者领进厨房，打开冰箱，拿出一条非常小的鱼："给你，吃饭时吃掉吧。"

第二天，记者又给巴里打电话。

巴里问她："你吃那条鱼了吗？"

"是的，我把鱼煎了。"

"很好，你今天感觉有什么不同吗？"

"没有。我认为这样一条小鱼，50美元有点太贵了。"

"太好了！"巴里说："你看，鱼起作用了，你现在已学会用脑子想问题了。"

feel *v.* 感觉

Lasting a Lifetime

Sidney Wilson's watch was old and it did not work well. It was either too fast or too slow. It spent more time in the *repair* shop than on his *wrist*. He decided to buy himself a new watch.

He went into a *jewelry* shop and spoke to the saleswoman behind the *counter*. "I want to buy a new

能用一辈子的手表

悉尼·威尔森的表旧了，又不好用，不是太快就是太慢。表在维修店的时间比戴在他手上的时间要多得多，因此他决定买块新手表。

他来到珠宝店对柜台售货员说："我想买块新表，请给我拿一块你们店里最好的表。"

---

repair *n.* 修理；修补
jewelry *n.* 首饰；珠宝
wrist *n.* 手腕
counter *n.* 柜台

watch please. Show me the best watch you have."

The saleswoman smiled happily. This was the kind of customer she liked.

"Certainly sir," she said, and showed Sidney a gold watch.

"This watch is made of gold and has twenty-four *jewels*," she explained.

"How much is it?" Sidney asked.

"5000 dollars," the saleswoman said.

"Oh," Sidney said. "I'm sorry. You did not understand me. I want to see the best watch you have for under $100."

The saleswoman now lost interest in Sidney. She pushed some cheap watches at him. "Choose one of these," she said *rudely*. "They are all under $100."

售货员高兴地笑着，她喜欢这样的顾客。

"好的，先生。"说完，她就递给悉尼一块金表。

"这块表是金制的，上面有24颗钻石。"她解释说。

"多少钱？"悉尼问。

"5000美元。"售货员回答。

"啊，"悉尼忙说，"很抱歉，你可能没听懂我的意思。我想看看你们店中100美元以下最好的表。"

售货员马上对悉尼失去了兴趣。她拿出一些便宜的表递给悉尼，然后极不礼貌地说："从这些表当中挑一块吧，它们都是100美元以下的。"

jewel n. 宝石　　　　　　　　　　　　rudely adv. 粗鲁地

CULTURE SERIES

Sidney *picked up* one of the watches, "Will it last me a lifetime?" he asked.

"Of course," the saleswoman said.

"Then I'll buy it," Sidney told her. He paid for the watch and left the shop.

Two days later, the watch stopped. Sidney could not make it start again. He took it back to the shop.

"This watch is *broken*," he said to the saleswoman. "You told me it would last me a lifetime."

"When you bought it, sir," the saleswoman said, "you didn't look very well."

悉尼拿起其中的一块表问道:"这表我能用一辈子吗?"

"当然能啦。"售货员回答。

"那我就买这块表了。"悉尼付款后就离开了商店。

两天后,表停了,悉尼怎么摆弄都不好用,于是他把表拿回了商店。

"这块表坏了,"他对营业员说,"你不是说这表可以用一辈子吗?"

"先生,你买表的时候," 营业员说,"看起来不是很健康啊。"

---

pick up 挑选　　　　　　　　　broken *adj.* 损坏的;出故障的